MACMILLAN MASTER GUIDES

General Editor: James Gibson

Published:

JANE AUSTEN: **PRIDE AND PREJUDICE** Raymond Wilson
　　　　　　EMMA Norman Page
　　　　　　MANSFIELD PARK Richard Wirdnam
ROBERT BOLT: **A MAN FOR ALL SEASONS** Leonard Smith
EMILY BRONTË: **WUTHERING HEIGHTS** Hilda D. Spear
GEOFFREY CHAUCER: **THE PROLOGUE TO THE CANTERBURY TALES**
　　　　　　Nigel Thomas and Richard Swan
　　　　　　THE MILLER'S TALE Michael Alexander

CHARLES DICKENS: **BLEAK HOUSE** Dennis Butts

GEO

E. M.

THE

WIL

OLI

THO

CHR

ART

GEO

WIL

GEO

RIC

Fort

SAM

WIL

GEO

T. S.

HEN

E. M

WIL

THO

SEL

PHI

D. H

HAR

THO

ART

WIL

TWO PLAYS O

Also published by Macmillan

MASTERING ENGLISH LITERATURE R. Gill
MASTERING ENGLISH LANGUAGE S. H. Burton
MASTERING ENGLISH GRAMMAR S. H. Burton

WORK OUT SERIES
WORK OUT ENGLISH LANGUAGE ('O' level and GCSE) S. H. Burton
WORK OUT ENGLISH LITERATURE ('A' level) S. H. Burton

MACMILLAN MASTER GUIDES

THE MILLER'S TALE

BY GEOFFREY CHAUCER

MICHAEL ALEXANDER

MACMILLAN

First edition 1986

Published by
MACMILLAN EDUCATION LTD
Houndmills, Basingstoke, Hampshire RG21 2XS
and London
Companies and representatives
throughout the world

Typeset by TecSet Ltd,
Sutton, Surrey

Printed in Hong Kong

British Library Cataloguing in Publication Data
Alexander, Michael
The miller's tale by Geoffrey Chaucer.–(Macmillan
master guides)
1. Chaucer, Geoffrey. Miller's tale
I. Title   II. Chaucer, Geoffrey, *1340–1400*.
Miller's tale
821'.1   PR1868.M6
ISBN 0-333-40258-8 Pbk
ISBN 0-333-40259-6 Pbk export

CONTENTS

GENERAL EDITOR'S PREFACE

The aim of the Macmillan Master Guides is to help you to appreciate the book you are studying by providing information about it and by suggesting ways of reading and thinking about it which will lead to a fuller understanding. The section on the writer's life and background has been designed to illustrate those aspects of the writer's life which have influenced the work, and to place it in its personal and literary context. The summaries and critical commentary are of special importance in that each brief summary of the action is followed by an examiniation of the significant critical points. The space which might have been given to repetitive explanatory notes has been devoted to a detailed analysis of the kind of passage which might confront you in an examination. Literary criticism is concerned with both the broader aspects of the work being studied and with its detail. The ideas which meet us in reading a great work of literature, and their relevance to us today, are an essential part of our study, and our Guides look at the thought of their subject in some detail. But just as essential is the craft with which the writer has constructed his work of art, and this may be considered under several technical headings — characterisation, language, style and stage-craft, for example.

The authors of these Guides are all teachers and writers of wide experience, and they have chosen to write about books they admire and know well in the belief that they can communicate their admiration to you. But you yourself must read and know intimately the book you are studying. No one can do that for you. You should see this book as a lamp-post. Use it to shed light, not to lean against. If you know your text and know what it is saying about life, and how it says it, then you will enjoy it, and there is no better way of passing an examination in literature.

JAMES GIBSON

ACKNOWLEDGEMENT

Cover illustration: Detail from *Pilgrimage to Canterbury* by Thomas Stothard (1806-7). ©Tate Gallery Publications.

1 GEOFFREY CHAUCER: LIFE AND BACKGROUND

1.1 CHAUCER'S LIFE

While we know a good deal about Geoffrey Chaucer's public career, we know little of his life and less of his personality. He was regarded by his successors as the best of English poets and eventually as the father of our poetry. Chaucer is not only a more complete but also a much more readable poet for us than his contemporaries, William Langland, the author of *Piers Plowman*, or the anonymous but perhaps even more remarkable author of *Pearl* and *Sir Gawain and the Green Knight*. But no scholar disputes that these contemporaries were gifted and serious poets; indeed, to those who know it, the reign of King Richard II (1377-99) may now seem quite as rich in poetry as that of any of his successors except Queen Elizabeth I and King James I. Much of merit survives from the period before Chaucer, in whose day English came to rival French as the vernacular literary language; and much of the verse in English from between the end of the Anglo-Saxon period and the fourteenth century was not written down or has not survived. The reason that, in mid-fourteenth-century England, writing in English suddenly came to rival that in French is that English itself suddenly triumphed in social life; in 1363 Parliament was summoned in English for the first time. Langland and the *Gawain* master were provincials and wrote in old-fashioned literary forms and in dialects which do not have the advantage of the ancestral relationship to modern English possessed by Chaucer's London English. Chaucer is superior but he is not an unprecedented nor an isolated phenomenon.

But if poetry is at all, as has been claimed, 'the breath and finer spirit of all knowledge', the modern non-specialist reader of English is likely to get his essential, perhaps his only, insight into the life of late mediaeval England, and of the mediaeval Christendom of which it was a part, through Chaucer rather than through Langland or John Gower or Jean Froissart or the surviving lyrics and plays. The Gothic cathedrals, and modern illustrated books on mediaeval art, are other direct sources for our ideas of the life of the Middle Ages.

Chaucer's career as a whole casts some light on his work as a whole but little on the *Miller's Tale*; which occupies eight of the 248 pages of the *Canterbury Tales* in the second edition of his *Works* by F. N. Robinson; the *Tales* themselves amounting to less than one-third of these *Works*. From the hundreds of mentions of Chaucer's name in the official records, not one alludes in any way to his poetic calling. He was a government servant and diplomat who held important offices of trust in a public career lasting a little over twenty years. His grandfather and father were Ipswich and London wine merchants who held minor office in the Royal household, and Geoffrey was born in London in the early 1340s. He was a page in a royal household and valet to King Edward III before entering the King's full-time public service. He was ransomed from captivity in France, where he had been fighting for the King, by Edward himself in 1360. Then he disappeared from view until 1366, when he went on a mission in Spain. In 1367 he went to France on the King's business, and he fought again in France in 1369. In 1372 he went to Genoa and Florence, and in 1378 to Milan, again on the King's business.

From 1374 he became Controller of Customs and Subsidy of Wools, Skins and Hides - England's chief trade; and was given a house over Aldgate, the east gate of the City of London. His public life is then well documented for ten prosperous years in this office, but in 1385 he withdrew into Kent and although he was a Member of Parliament and a Justice of the Peace thereafter, he held only one important office, being Clerk of the King's Works, 1389-91, responsible for the upkeep of the Tower, Westminster Hall and St George's Chapel, Windsor, as well as the Palace of Westminster itself. Thereafter he held the office of the forestership of North Petherton, Somerset, probably a sinecure. Most of these records are of grants and annuities, which were renewed by King Henry IV on his accession in 1399. Chaucer rented a house in the garden of Westminster Abbey in December of that year; he died on 25 October 1400 and was buried in the Abbey, an honour accorded to only one commoner before him. Recognition of his poetry came before his death.

Of his private life we know nothing, though there are intriguing features to his family history. His mother and his father's mother each married three times. His wife, Philippa Payne Roet, whom he married in or before 1367, was the elder sister of Katharine Swynford, later the mistress and eventually the wife of John of Gaunt, the uncle of King Richard II and the greatest noble in England. Philippa probably died in 1387 and they probably had at least two sons, Thomas and Lowys. A daughter (or sister) of Geoffrey became a nun. He appeared in law cases which are difficult to interpret, and was sued for debt, but no personal light is cast by the records. Two incidents revealing of the life of the time are that in 1390 he was attacked and robbed three times in four days; and there is a later report of a record that he was fined two shillings while he was a law student at the Inner Temple for 'beating a Franciscan friar in Fleet Street'. In his poetry Chaucer portrays his mature self as always reading books, comically puzzled by Love, rather plump, and with an 'elvyssh' countenance. There is a famous 'frontispiece' to a manuscript of Chaucer's *Troilus and Criseyde* which shows the poet reading to the court of King Richard II.

From these records and the evidence of the poetry we can tell only that Chaucer was a trusted royal and public servant, of merchant family, who had a varied career and knew the men of his day in all walks of life – kings, noblemen and ladies, merchants, lawyers, scholars and writers, scientists, religious laymen, and also men of affairs of every sort, high and low. He kept out of trouble in troublesome times and lived to be old.

Features of his career which might conceivably bear on the *Miller's Tale* are his mercantile background and his work in customs and diplomacy, all of which would have accustomed him to the tricks people get up to. He once detected a merchant who tried to export wool without paying duty, and was accordingly paid the resulting fine of £71 4s 6d. His work as a surveyor might have increased his ability to describe a building: John's house in Oxford, the scene of the *Tale*, is given in great physical detail. In *Chaucer at Oxford and Cambridge* (Oxford, 1974) J. A. W. Bennett reproduces a reconstruction of this house; he also shows how well Chaucer knew Oxford and how many friends he had among the academics, especially at Merton College. Fascinating though all this is to our curiosity, its relation to the *Tale* is not certain.

1.2 BACKGROUND AND CONTEXT

The *Canterbury Tales* is an unfinished work. In the *General Prologue* the pilgrims meeting at the Tabard Inn, Southwark, agree to the Host's proposal that they should each tell two tales on the way to Canterbury and two on the way back to Southwark. Chaucer had not even completed the first round of thirty tales when he provided what is clearly meant as a conclusion to the work with the *Parson's Tale*, told towards evening but short of Canterbury. In the manuscripts the completed tales fall into groups or fragments, within which tales are linked, but the fragments themselves are not linked to each other. Two or three orders have been proposed for the fragments. The largest fragment is Fragment A, also known as Fragment 1 or the First Fragment, of 4422 lines, containing the *Prologue* (also known as the *General Prologue*), the *Knight's Tale*, the *Miller's Tale*, the *Reeve's Tale*, the *Cook's Tale* (incomplete) and their respective prologues or headlinks. Thus the *Miller's Tale* has as much surrounding matter as any of the *Canterbury Tales*, and this immediate context is valuable for the modern reader, helping us to get several bearings on the *Miller's Tale* and to study it more securely, even if we read it in isolation.

What are the chief bearings provided by this body of text surrounding the *Miller's Tale*? It is a tale told by a pilgrim introduced and described in the *General Prologue*, as most of the tales are. The portrait of the Miller is vivid and rather explicit: he is clearly going to be a source of trouble. His profession, and the company he keeps among the pilgrims, also tell us a good deal.

The *Miller's Prologue* or Headlink confirms that he is drunk, indecorous, a bully and a tease, motivated by resentment against the nobility of the *Knight's Tale*, impatience towards the authority of the Host as master of the tale-telling game, and aggression towards the Reeve. He wishes to *quite* (requite, answer, match) the *Knight's Tale*, of which indeed his own tale turns out to be a parody. Finally, the quarrel he has begun with the Reeve (who is also a carpenter) is pursued after the *Miller's Tale* in the *Reeve's Prologue* and his *Tale*, which avenges the Miller's insult to the marital honour of carpenters by relating the double cuckolding of a Miller.

The *Canterbury Tales* also offers other contexts for the *Miller's Tale* in that it includes other tales of the same low comic type, known as the *fabliau*, a form with conventions almost amounting to rules (see Section 2.2 on page 16). Likewise, the *Tales* as a whole contain quarrels similar to those which the Miller picks with the Knight, the Host and the Reeve, based on social or sexual jealousy or trade rivalry or conflicting ideals. The *Tales* also offer many examples of the dramatic or thematic relationship between a teller and his tale. These comparisons will be pursued later.

1.3 THE FRAME-STORY

All but one of the *Canterbury Tales* are told by pilgrims, nearly all of whom are described at some length in the *General Prologue*. The Miller's portrait leads us to expect that he might tell a rough and bawdy story, and so he does. Chaucer must have thought of the pilgrimage as a *frame-story* in order to introduce tales he had already written or already wanted to write. Two other famous collections of tales in the literature of the world are mediaeval and also have frame-stories: the Arabian *Thousand and One Nights*, where the Princess Scheherezade has to beguile the Shah by telling him a story which keeps him awake all night. It is she who tells all the stories and her character and situation do not change. In Giovanni Boccaccio's *Decameron* (a title derived from the Greek for ten days) ten young people sheltering from the Black Death outside Florence each tell one story per day for ten days. But their characters are not always distinct and they themselves do not interact dramatically, as Chaucer's tellers do. In the *Arabian Nights* or the *Decameron*, or in the *Novelle* (Tales) of Giovanni Sercambi, a fourteenth-century collection which is also set on a pilgrimage, the frame-story exists for the sake of the tales it includes. Chaucer's characters, by contrast, interact and reveal their natures in doing so. It has been said that the Pilgrimage, the story of the pilgrims on the road, is the best tale in the *Canterbury Tales*. It is certainly fascinating, if incomplete, and its general outline is clear enough: it is a story of mounting social and moral chaos, called to sudden order by the Parson's reminder to the pilgrims of the purpose of their communal activity: penance.

1.4 THE TELLERS

Between the tales some of the pilgrims climb down out of their wall-paintings in the *General Prologue* and begin to speak, act and interact very vigorously. The Miller is the first to do so. He has led the pilgrims out of town with his bagpipes, and he then disrupts the Host's plans; in doing so he no doubt offends others besides the Reeve. Some critics have been so taken with the vehement speech and strong reactions among the pilgrims before and after the tales, that for them the pilgrims become primary and the tales secondary. The interest of the tale would then be as a revelation of the character of its teller. This is more plausible in the case of the Pardoner, who has a long, autobiographical prologue and an epilogue in which he is angrily exposed as a fake by the Host.

The Wife of Bath, too, has a long, self-exposing prologue. Many tales are well suited to their tellers, and some indeed are revealing. But others are unsuited to their tellers and evidently in the process of being adapted by Chaucer. In general, however, those critics who find the tellers more real than the tales, and read the tales as personal disclosures, are over-responding to a brilliant illusory realism which is only one of Chaucer's modes of writing. They are imposing on Chaucer a modern way of understanding derived from our reading of novels, which purport to present the behaviour of actual individuals. The tales, it is clear, preceded their tellers and the tales remain primary. Thus, the character of the Miller is a key to reading his tale rather than the other way round. Although the study of the *Miller's Tale* in isolation is therefore legitimate and proper, it is also right to glean what we can from its setting.

1.5 THE TALE AND THE *TALES*

The relationship of the *Miller's Tale* to the *Canterbury Tales* as a whole is very hard to assess, as the work is incomplete. Twenty-four stories are told in all, two of them by Chaucer. Four of the tales told are themselves incomplete or interrupted. The order of the fragments is still debated. Some scholars now think the Hengwrt manuscript superior to the Ellesmere manuscript followed by F. N. Robinson (and J. Winny). The value of sketching a context for the *Miller's Tale* beyond the First Fragment in which it is set is therefore somewhat general.

The *Tales* as a whole, however, do exhibit several characteristics to be found in this tale. They are varied, even miscellaneous. Besides the *fabliaux* described on page 16, there are many pious and moral tales, those of the Man of Law, the Clerk, the Physician, the Pardoner, the Prioress, Chaucer (the *Meliboeus*), the Monk, the Second Nun, the Manciple and the Parson. There are romances such as those told by the Wife of Bath, the Squire, the Franklin, and (in parody form) Chaucer (*Sir Thopas*). The linking material of the pilgrimage frame-story is full of lively, often comic, exchanges. There are many tales which fit into two or three categories, and there are multiple perspectives upon the action and themes of the pilgrimage and its tale-telling game. There are beast-fables, allegories, saints' lives, tragedies, fairy stories, sermons and scurrilous tales. Among the themes canvassed are the nature of marriage and the honesty and honour of various professions, secular and religious. The tone and mood of the *Tales* varies from solemn, earnest, pious and pathetic to gay, worldly and witty, and to ribald and angry. The proportion of more serious tales rises towards the end, and the *Parson's Tale*, a treatise on penitence, is followed in most manuscripts by a formal 'Retracciouns' in which Chaucer 'retracts' those tales which tend towards sin.

Against this colourfully mixed background, the *Miller's Tale* can assume a variety of aspects. It can be argued that since Chaucer achieved no unity of design or view in the *Tales*, each tale is best taken on its own without regard to a presumed master-plan. On the whole, the effect of reading the *Tales* through in sequence (something Chaucer himself may not have done as often as modern scholars) is to diminish confidence that any simple 'interpretation' was intended either of the whole or of each part. The desire for such a key is not surprising in readers today, when every writer may have his own view of the world, but this may not be the best approach to the products of an age where there was a far greater common understanding of the purposes of life, an understanding grounded in theology. Nothing in the *Canterbury Tales* as a whole recommends the notion that any single self-contained answer can be given to the examination question 'What does the *Miller's Tale* mean?' On the contrary, one might expect it to 'mean' several things.

2 SUMMARY AND CRITICAL COMMENTARY

2.1 SUMMARY

The *Miller's Portrait*

In the *General Prologue* Chaucer describes the company of twenty-nine pilgrims he meets at the Tabard Inn in a series of portraits arranged roughly in descending social order, which is also roughly a descending moral order. After the military and religious pilgrims come what we might call the bourgeois; then follow two virtuous brothers, the Parson and the Plowman, who love their neighbours as themselves. The Miller's is the first portrait in the final group; he is found with the Manciple, Reeve, Summoner and Pardoner. The first two, a domestic bursar and an estate manager, are lay stewards; the latter pair, an official of the bishop's court and a seller of fake indulgences, are ecclesiastical stewards; all four are corrupt parasites.

The Miller is described as big and strong, a champion wrestler and door-smasher; hairy and warty; well-armed and foul-mouthed; dishonest in his trade and prosperous; a player of the bagpipes. For commentary and critical analysis see 2.2.

The *Miller's Prologue*

After the *Knight's Tale*, the Host of the Tabard invites the Monk to tell the next story. According to the rules of the game, to which the pilgrims have agreed at the end of the *General Prologue*, the Host is in sole charge of the proceedings. We have already seen him arrange that it is the Knight who begins the tale-telling game. The Host wants the Monk to continue after the Knight because 'Sir Monk' is the next pilgrim in order of social precedence, and this will lend further respectability to the Host's scheme. The Host's smooth stage-management is disrupted by the Miller, who is drunk. It may be imagined that he cannot bear hearing the *Knight's Tale* so generally praised as noble and memorable, especially by the *gentils*. He will tell them a tale which shows them what love is really like, not a lot of airy-fairy nonsense far away and long ago. He brushes aside the Host's protest that he is drunk, blaming any mistakes in his speech on the quality of the ale served by the Host; and announces that he will tell how a student cuckolded a carpenter. The Reeve (a carpenter) protests, but the Miller elaborately explains that he had never meant to imply that the Reeve himself was a cuckold. The unstoppable Miller proceeds to tell the story, Chaucer apologising for repeating obscenities (1-78).

The *Miller's Tale*

Once there was a rich old carpenter living in Oxford who took in lodgers. His lodger was Nicholas, a poor arts student, quite a charmer, who had turned to astrology to make a living. John the carpenter had recently married a girl of eighteen whom he loved more than his life but kept under his jealous eye: Alisoun was extremely attractive, and knew it (79-162).

Nicholas made advances to Alisoun and she agreed to sleep with him if Nicholas could devise a plan to beguile John (163-98). The parish clerk, Absolon, who fancied himself as a lady-killer, also fancied Alisoun. One night he sang a serenade outside her window, and wooed her in every way he could, but to no avail for she loved Nicholas (199-290).

Nicholas shut himself up in his room all one Saturday and Sunday. John became alarmed: his servant reported that he could spy Nicholas sitting motionless, staring up into the air. They broke into the room and Nicholas told John, under an oath of secrecy, what the stars had revealed to him: that on Monday night the world would be drowned by a second Flood. But (Nicholas further revealed) John, like Noah in the Old Testament, could save himself, Alisoun and Nicholas by building an ark, or rather three little arks, one each. It must all be kept a secret, and when they were in their arks they must not even speak to one another (291-492).

John hung three tubs in the roof, and sent his servants away. He built a little ladder for each ark. The three of them climbed up and said goodnight, and John, who was exhausted, fell asleep waiting for the rain. Nicholas and Alisoun crept down to the carpenter's bed and gleefully made love all night (493-548).

Absolon had heard that John had not been seen and might be away. He went before dawn on Tuesday to the carpenter's window and begged Alisoun for a kiss. She said she loved another but would give him a kiss if he would go away. Alisoun stuck her bottom out of the window and in the darkness the kneeling Absolon kissed her naked arse. Furious at the laughter he could hear within, he vowed revenge (549–638).

Absolon borrowed a hot coulter from Gervase the Smith and returned to the window. He offered Alisoun a gold ring in return for another kiss. This time it was Nicholas who stuck his bottom out of the window. He farted at Absolon but Absolon struck him with the hot coulter, burning off a lot of skin. Nicholas cried out: 'Help! Water! Water! Help!' (639–707).

The cry of 'Water!' awoke John, who cut the ropes, expecting his little ark to settle gently on the waters of the Flood. It fell to the ground, the fall knocking him out and breaking his arm. The young lovers rushed out into the street to raise the alarm. When John tried to explain his fall they told the neighbours that John had had a mad fantasy about a second Noah's Flood and that they had joined him in the roof only to humour him. Everyone agreed, amid laughter, that the carpenter was mad (708–46).

2.2 CRITICAL COMMENTARY

The Miller's portrait

There was a standard way of describing a physical figure, recommended to writers in mediaeval rhetorical handbooks. Chaucer refers to these books, but he may have learned more of how to do this by reading and imitation. He began writing by translating *Le Roman de la Rose*, the thirteenth-century French masterpiece. In this the Dreamer falls asleep and finds himself outside a country park, on the wall of which allegorical personages are depicted from top to toe. Some trace of this tradition of physical description may be found in the portraits in the *Prologue*, which remain in their conception formal and self-contained, despite the haphazard and impromptu air with which the pilgrim Chaucer delivers them. Chaucer generally mentions face and physique, clothes and profession, manner and conversation, though he varies the proportions in each portrait. Idealistic pilgrims, like the Parson, are described by their ideals, materialistic pilgrims, like the Miller, materialistically.

Physiognomy was in mediaeval times a moral art, a guide to character, and the Miller's physique is described in unprecedented detail. He is 'a stout carl' and a champion wrestler, and 'Ful big he was of brawn and eek of bones'; more specifically 'He was short-sholdred, brood, a thikke knarre [knot of wood]'. His beard was red and broad, and on the top of his nose he had a wart sprouting red hair. He had black nostrils and a great big mouth. To a powerful physique Chaucer has added a concentrated impression of the Miller's face.

Thus the Miller's physical presence is vividly established, and we are now told that he is a keen and successful wrestler, strong enough to lift any door off its hinges or to smash any door by running at it with his head. He carries a sword and shield. He is an incessant talker and teller of jokes and stories, mostly dirty stories. He is a lusty player of the bagpipes. He also is a successfully dishonest miller.

In mediaeval times, more than today, a man's profession identified him and moulded his character. All the pilgrims are described in terms of their trade or calling. Each is typical of his profession - the fat hunting monk, the *gentil* knight, the ladylike prioress, the *bisy* lawyer, the clipped clerk, the pompous guildsmen. The doctor is the best doctor in the world. The Yeoman is called 'yeomanlike'. And the Miller is everyone's idea of a miller. The scholar W. P. Ker was once walking in Switzerland with an undergraduate student, who asked him to identify a passing bird. 'That is a woodcock,' replied Ker. 'It is not my idea of a woodcock,' said the student. 'It is God's idea of a woodcock,' said Ker. Chaucer's portrait gives us God's idea of a miller.

Millers were often unpopular because they stood between a man and his own bread: they had the monopoly of grinding corn in a neighbourhood; on a manorial estate the mill was the only place where growers were permitted to have their corn ground, and millers were commonly suspected of abusing their position by overcharging and of not handing over all the flour at the end of the grinding process. Chaucer tells us of his miller that he knew well how to steal corn and to charge three times over for it. The dishonesty of millers was so proverbial that it was said that an honest miller has a golden thumb (that is, there are no honest millers). Chaucer, in his narrator's role as a naïve pilgrim, exclaims with wonder that despite his dishonesty this miller actually had a golden thumb - that is, he had become prosperous by putting his thumb in the scale when weighing out the flour. The German proverb is: 'The miller is honest who has hair on his teeth.'

Mills

Wind and water mills were not in the fourteenth century the picturesque adornments to a sleepy countryside which they have been since the English landscape painters of East Anglia discovered them in the nineteenth century. They were a fairly recent and highly successful piece of technology. A mill was, after the church and the lord's house, the largest building in a village. A windmill was the largest machine that most of the population, nearly all of whom lived on the land, would ever see. At the end of the Middle Ages Cervantes' Don Quixote tilted at windmills, mistaking them for the giants that a knight errant was supposed to slay. And they must have sometimes seemed, revolving on their bases as well as whirling their sails or 'arms', frighteningly gigantic. Undoubtedly the Miller's characteristic activities are derived from his mill: mastering, grinding, breaking, crushing, flailing – and talking. Those who talked too much, like the Wife of Bath, were said to 'clap as a mill', which makes a continuous noise. The Reeve tells the Miller (in his *Prologue*) to 'stint his clap' (hold his tongue). (The miller described in the *Reeve's Tale* makes a continuous noise, like his water mill, even when asleep.) Likewise, windmills were made entirely or principally of wood, and there is an immense amount of wood in the *Miller's Tale*. Even in the Portrait the Miller's strength is attested by his ability to unhinge or smash doors, however huge. Millers had to be strong, in order to lift sacks and move heavy beams, and this Miller is the local strong man and wrestling champion. Wrestling (a very popular activity in mediaeval England) was often used in art as an image of discord; another common image of discord (also of lechery) was the bagpipes. The Miller leading the pilgrims out of town with his noisy bagpipes does not augur well for the social harmony of this professedly holy band.

Imagery

But the Miller's physique, activities and trade, eloquent though they are, tell us less than the imagery Chaucer uses to suggest his nature. He won the *ram* at wrestling matches; his beard was as red as the hair of *any sow or fox*; the hairs on the wart on the top of his nose are *as red as the bristles of a sow's ears*. Taken together with the brawn and bones, these suggest bestial affinities. The ram is famous for its strength in charging and battering; the sow for corpulence, sloth and filth; the fox for cunning and stealth. All three animals have prominent snouts. Immediately after the sow's ears (or arse, the spelling is ambiguous), we hear that the Miller's nostrils were black and wide, while his mouth was as large as a large furnace. The black nostrils and red mouth add a voracious and slightly demonic finishing touch to a distinctly feral and menacing mug-shot. The close-up and the magnification of unattractive physical detail are still the stock-in-trade of the caricaturist; hostile political cartoons still employ the bestial analogies which (however unfair they may seem to modern animal-lovers) we inherit from ancestors more familiar with animals than we are.

At a first reading the Miller's portrait may seem merely more vivid and more vigorously animated than those of his predecessors in the gallery of pilgrims. The microscopic examination given above may seem to 'read in' an unintended moral significance to an apparently casual sketch. But the Miller is not even described as 'a good fellow' (Chaucer's minimum compliment in the *Prologue*); he is the first pilgrim to be criticised openly and frankly – he is called dishonest and foul-mouthed. He is a rascal and not a particularly appealing or amiable one, though Chaucer clearly enjoys the vigour of speech of his 'stout churl'. He pretends that he does not like repeating the Miller's bawdy language, but this is a conventional disclaimer, an amusingly transparent excuse.

There has grown up a modern tradition of apparent moral neutrality in the arts: it is the duty of the artist or writer to hold a mirror up to nature, to show life as it is and without comment – 'warts and all', as Oliver Cromwell, the plain-spoken ruler of England after the Civil War in the seventeenth century, is said to have told Sir Peter Lely, his portrait-painter. But the very instruction admits the well-known fact that facial warts have never been considered attractive. Chaucer did not know of the modern preference for the appearance of moral neutrality, nor that things should be depicted not in black and white but only in shades of grey: his world is highly coloured and dramatic, with an implied heaven at the top and a hell, like a great furnace, at the bottom. In a universe with such a polarity, nothing is merely neutral or neuter. Physiognomy was moral as well as scientific, and the details of the Miller's face have a more than physiological significance. The description is not in proportion but progressively exaggerated: the Miller's wart is right on the top of his nose; and right on the top of the wart is a tuft of hairs; and these hairs are as red as the bristles in a sow's ears. A glance at a sow's ear confirms Chaucer's accuracy. But this is a caricature, not a close-up photograph: Chaucer is not interested only in the colour of the Miller's hair but also in the other connotations of sow's ears. The old English proverb (first recorded in the sixteenth century) says that you cannot make a silk purse out of a sow's ear. This is usually a way of saying that clothes cannot make a gentleman out of a boor, but the point is that a sow's ear was proverbial for something irremediably hairy. The Miller's portrait is a vivid moral emblem as well as a brilliantly realised description.

The beastliness of the Miller also has social connotations. Hairiness is a reminder of the animal part of our nature, then considered to be very much less noble than the intellectual part. The fourteenth century saw an increasing refinement of manners at Court. Chaucer's lifetime included the founding of the Order of the Garter and also of Winchester College, with their noble mottoes: *Honi soit qui mal y pense* (Shame on him who thinks ill thereof) and 'Manners Makyth Man'. The Order of the Garter, an order of chivalry, was founded by King Edward III when, the story goes, the King stooped in a dance to pick up the garter of the young Countess of Salisbury, and made this celebrated retort to criticism. Chaucer was personally ransomed from French captivity by Edward III. The poet probably also knew the founder of Winchester College, William of Wykeham (1324–1404), bishop of Winchester and Chancellor of England, whose first employment was as Clerk of the King's Works at Windsor, a post later held by Chaucer. The social and moral gulf between the teller of the previous tale, the 'parfit gentil' knight, who was never rude to anyone, and the churlish Miller, was marked. There was a contemporary debate upon the nature of *gentilesse* (true nobility), which was agreed to be spiritual and moral rather than inherited and genetic; but this theory had to contend with the facts of feudal subordination and power. Hairiness was feral, not noble, a mark of the Miller's coarseness.

The Miller's prologue

This heading is the suggestion of a modern editor. The manuscript reads 'Heere folwen the wordes bitwene the Hoost and the Millere' and what follows is indeed an exchange of words rather than any kind of formal prologue by the Miller. The *gentils*' reception of the *Knight's Tale* pleases the Host, who is shown at some length in the *General Prologue*. He is 'a manly man' (like the Monk, and the Miller) and fit to be 'a marshall in an halle'. He has successfully persuaded the pilgrims to accept his overlordship on their way to Canterbury and ensured that they shall dine at his inn, the Tabard, on their return.

The Miller rudely interrupts the next stage of the plan by which the Host observes social precedence, as innkeepers and marshals are wont to do, by inviting the Monk to follow the Knight. This interruption is the first obviously dramatic moment in the *Canterbury Tales*; it is only in retrospect that the Host's original high-jacking of the Pilgrimage is seen to have been crucial. The Host's jocular fixing of the draw at the end of the *General Prologue* and his swearing suggest some indecorum, but do not prepare us for the farcical outrage of the Miller's smashing entrance on to the scene of the action. So drunk (at this early hour of the day) that he can hardly sit on his horse, he'll give way to no man and roars out oaths in *Pilate's voice*. (This is the first of Chaucer's three explicit references to the popular Miracle or Mystery plays, in which Pontius

Pilate, the Roman governor who condemned Jesus to death, was played as a ranting, raving character.) The Miller's opening words swear by the arms, blood and bones of Christ (at the Crucifixion), an eloquent if blasphemous expression of his impatience at the prospect of further *gentils* and their *noble* tales.

The Host, who is experienced in these matters, sees that the Miller is drunk, but unfortunately suggests that *some better man* should tell the next tale. The Miller passionately declares that if he can't tell the next tale he'll go away. The Host petulantly surrenders his authority in order to save the face of his scheme. All the dignity, harmony and order of the *Knight's Tale*, and of the pilgrims, are lost, and the *Canterbury Tales* begins to reveal its dramatic variety. It is clear that the mood has totally changed, but we do not yet know what to expect.

Having got his way, the Miller changes from drunken anger to broad comedy. He is so far gone in drink that he proudly claims to know that he is drunk by the way his voice sounds; any mispronunciations or blunders in what he says are therefore to be blamed on the poor quality of the Host's ale. This drunken logic is as good as anything in Shakespeare's tavern scenes. The joking continues with the Miller's claim that his tale of how a *clerk* (student) has made a fool (and by implication a cuckold) of a carpenter is to be *a legende and a lyf*, that is the life of a saint or martyr.

The Reeve's immediate reply suggests that he feels threatened by such a tale, and reminds us that he was a carpenter by trade. A reeve was the bailiff or factor for an estate – today's estate-manager. Any reeve might have a conflict of interest with a miller on his estate since the operations of millers were difficult to control. (Carpenters and millers did not always get on well either.) This reeve is described in the *General Prologue* as dishonest, like the Miller, but also, unlike the Miller, discreet and apparently deferential to his lord, though secretly harsh to underlings. He is a *sclendre, colerik* man and rides last of the pilgrims, at the greatest possible distance from the huge, brawling, bagpipe-playing Miller.

The choleric nature of the Reeve is borne out by his tone, which undermines the undoubted moral sense of what he says and suggests his uneasiness. The Miller seizes on this shrillness of tone and, with a leering sarcasm which is so excessive that it becomes comic, explains that he had never said that the Reeve was married, still less a cuckold. Against the charge that he was slandering women, the Miller replies that it is well known that there are hardly any bad women. He is married himself and does not suppose that *he* is a cuckold. A man should not be too inquisitive into God's secrets nor into his wife's secrets - these are to be themes of his tale. He makes the vulgar suggestion that if a man gets enough sex from his wife he shouldn't worry about what else she may or may not be doing.

Chaucer elaborately apologises for the churlish tale which, as reporter, he is now obliged to repeat unless he is to deceive us. He has a similar apology at the end of the *General Prologue*, and at the end of manuscripts of the *Canterbury Tales* he retracts all the dirty stories he has told. Here he forgets that he is a pilgrim orally repeating what he has heard and (in line 69) advises those who don't want to hear the *Miller's Tale* to *turn over the leaf* and choose a more edifying tale, of which there are many - if they look carefully. His final warning is that we should not take a joke too seriously.

What has been the effect of the *Miller's Prologue*? It has revealed that the *Canterbury Tales* is to be not a smoothly-ordered pageant but may contain reversals of tone and subject from nobility to bawdy, and that the action of the frame-story may include violent quarrels among the lower orders, reflecting rivalries based not only on conflicts of professional interest but also on insults to masculine vanity. The *Knight's Tale* had included some marked changes of tone and some violent reversals of expectation, but it had ended in an effort at human order and dignity. It was not told *against* another pilgrim, and revealed little about its teller. From the *Miller's Prologue* onwards we no longer know what to expect in the *Canterbury Tales* as a whole. It does give us a good idea, however, of what to expect in the *Miller's Tale*.

The *Miller's Tale*: a fabliau

The *Miller's Tale* is what is known as a *fabliau*, a French literary form. The word *fabliau* comes from the Picard form of the Old French *fableau*, a little fable. It was originally a verse tale of the twelfth and thirteenth centuries. The *fabliaux* flourished in the Picard towns in northern France, and in Flanders and Holland. There are also many of them in the famous collection of prose tales, the *Decameron*, by the fourteenth-century Florentine writer Giovanni Boccaccio. As a literary form, the *fabliau* is normally a gross naturalistic and comic poem, and characteristically depicted comic persons and gross acts in an apparently realistic way. The persons and places are often bourgeois, that is, of the *bourg*, burgh or borough: townees, such as merchants, artisans and priests. It was once thought that the *fabliaux* were a product of the new bourgeois class emerging in the towns which prospered so notably in these parts of Europe. It now seems clear that they are not by but *about* the bourgeois, who are seen from the unflattering point of view of Court or university – satiric rather than edifying. It was only with the rise of the novel after the Reformation that stories of the bourgeoisie became edifying.

Chaucer is almost the only English writer to use the *fabliau* form. The central incident of a *fabliau* is essentially indecent, and learned authorities would ascribe this to a folk-tale origin. But the setting is always full of realistic modern details, as in fifteenth-century Dutch painting. The *Reeve's Tale* is set in a mill near Cambridge, where two Cambridge students, given North-of-England accents, revenge them- selves on the bullying miller who cheats them of their corn, by making love to his wife and his daughter in his own bedroom while he is asleep. The *Shipman's Tale* is set in a merchant's house in Paris, where a monk enjoys the favours of the merchant's wife in exchange for a hundred franks, which the foolish merchant has kindly lent him. The *Merchant's Tale* is set in another rich merchant's house, in northern Italy, where again the blind husband provides the means for his own cuckolding, helping his wife up into a pear tree where her lover (his squire) is wait- ing for her. The *Cook's Tale* starts off with a London apprentice who lodges with a friend whose wife is a prostitute. . . . There are also *fabliau* elements in the *Friar's Tale*. These bald summaries indicate the kind of action expected in a *fabliau*.

Thus the opening lines of the *Miller's Tale* tell us what to expect: *a riche gnof* who has a lodger will in a *fabliau* have an attractive young wife; and, if he lives in a university town, his lodger will be a clever student. The outcome is not in doubt, the only question is, by what ruse will the young outwit the old.

The plot

Nicholas is an astrologer, and it is by this dubious art that he tricks his host. The narrative excellence of a *fabliau* lies in the tallness of the story spun by the cunning young seducer, and the corresponding gullibility of his old victim. The story of a second Noah's Flood is tall enough to amuse us, and Chaucer lavishes his fantasy on adorning it. But the special excellence of the plot in the *Miller's Tale* is given by the artful combina- tion of a second plot, involving a second suitor, the silly Absolon. The second sub-plot is quite unnecessary to the action: Chaucer could easily have found some other device to send John crashing down. But the cry of *water* is cleverly led up to by the farcical antics at the window, which are so ludicrously indecent that in our curiosity to see Absolon's revenge we forget all about John hanging up in the roof.

The characters

Characterisation in a *fabliau* is secondary to plot and action. Although superficially realistic in setting and language, the *fabliau* is essentially an absurd fantasy machine designed to produce a trick climax. The characters are stock types and have no true character; they are better called figures. The recipe demands one rich, old, jealous husband, one attractive young wife, one cunning young seducer trusted by the husband; put all three in the same house and leave to cook. Chaucer adds Absolon, a foolish suitor, and creates a much more interesting situation, a double mousetrap where one word springs both traps. Although secondary, the characterisation is famously successful in the *Miller's Tale*, so that (as with the portrait of the Miller himself) we forget that the figures are types.

Exposition (lines 79-112)

Chaucer cleverly introduces us to Alisoun, who is the hub of the story, her old husband and her young lover in reverse order. The husband, John, a *riche gnof* who took in lodgers, was a carpenter. Given the Miller's preface (lines 34-5), we know that the Oxford lodger will be a student (a *clerk* was a student nominally in training for holy orders, as were all students) and that he will make a fool of the *wright* (carpenter) with his *wyf* (as yet unmentioned). *Gnof* is a word extinct in English but not in Scots, where *gnaf* (pronounced *nyáf*) is still a common term of contempt for a useless person. (Absolon, had he lived in modern Scotland, would have been a *wee gnaf*.) The carpenter is *riche* whereas his lodger, Nicholas, is *poure*, in this like the Clerk of Oxenford in the *General Prologue*, whose portrait makes a striking contrast in every other respect with that of Nicholas.

The Clerk of Oxenford is a serious student of philosophy who spends all the money he can get on books, which he keeps *at his beddes heed* – where Nicholas keeps his astrological equipment: his bed's head is laid out like an altar consecrated to astrology. Of the Clerk of Oxenford we are told in the *General Prologue*:

> For him was levere have at his beddes heed
> Twenty bokes, clad in blak or reed
> Of Aristotle and his philosophye
> Than robes riche, or fithele, or gay sautrye.

The *beddes heed* rhyming with *reed*, the *bokes* and the *gay sautrye* are common to both Oxford students, which underlines their differences;

these continue into their attitudes to money. The Clerk has no money:

> But al be that he was a philosophre
> Yet hadde he but litel gold in cofre;
> But al that he might of his freendes hente,
> On bokes and on lerning he it spente,
> And bisily gan for the soules preye
> Of hem that yaf him wherwith to scoleye.

The Clerk is a logician and a philosopher, here jokingly associated with alchemy through the so-called 'philosopher's stone' by which alchemists sought to turn base metals into gold; in which the Clerk is not interested. Astrology was in the fourteenth century a more respectable science than alchemy, but both 'arts' could be turned to profit, as by Nicholas here and the alchemist in Chaucer's *Canon's Yeoman's Tale*. Both were, for the orthodox, perversions of the intellect. The Clerk himself repays the friends who give him money for books by praying for their souls. Nicholas likewise lives off his friends, without praying for them, but he has a private income and also makes money out of astrology.

We are given no picture of John, and Nicholas is described by his character and activities rather than his physique. He is first established as an astrologer. Astrology is today a popular pseudo-science concerned with nativities – how exactly the heavens stood when the customer was born – and somewhat discredited in favour of another popular pseudo-science, psychology. Stars are now studied by astronomers, who are not concerned with how the stars influence those 'born under' them. The modern distinction between astrology and astronomy (that is, between beliefs about the influence of the stars, and the science of their movements) dates from the Renaissance, but there was a great interest in both aspects of the subject in Chaucer's day, particularly at Oxford, and certainly in the work of Chaucer himself, who wrote a *Treatise on the Astrolabe* and made many references to the stars. In the *Knight's Tale* both Palamon and Arcite blame the stars for their misfortunes, but Christian teaching naturally regarded such fatalism as pagan. Nevertheless the stars played an influential, if not determining, part in the way educated mediaeval people regarded events and character.

It is not clear how seriously Chaucer took astrology, but in this tale it is used purely for comic purposes. The Miller himself is not too sure of his astrological terms: in lines 85–90 he is, perhaps drunkenly, mocking the jargon. Chaucer makes particular mention of Nicholas's pretended ability to foretell showers, an apparently random example of what Nicholas could predict. These chance touches often turn out to be as carefully calculated as the choice of a word in the most artful of modern poets. The same may be said of *hende* and *Lyk a maiden* as epithets for Nicholas; of the running comparison with the unworldly Clerk of Oxenford; and of Nicholas's pervasive *sweetness*. (His rival, Absolon, strives obsessively to have sweet breath, which is one of the most compelling attractions of Alisoun herself. Sweetness of breath must have been less usual before recent improvements in oral and dental hygiene.) Nicholas can afford to live on his own, a mark of a liking for privacy which was thought suspicious in the Middle Ages. The *gay psaltery*, a stringed instrument like a small harp or zither, was evidently a suitable instrument for a sophisticated student less serious than the Clerk, somewhat like a guitar today. At this stage the gaiety of Nicholas's music adds a certain vigour to his description. However, since Chaucer makes much of this music, it may well turn out to be a clue, and we must watch for any recurrence.

The Carpenter's marriage (lines 113-24)
The opening lines (113-6) make explicit what the opening of the story has implied, that a jealous old husband will not succeed in locking up a wild young wife. The six lines of comment that follow are of a sort characteristic of Chaucer, as much as of the Miller: if you are so foolish as to break well-known rules, you have to take the consequences. He was asking for it, as we might say. Dionysius Cato was the author of a set of moralising proverbs widely popular in the Middle Ages.

His wife (lines 125-62)
The famous description of the carpenter's young wife is treated factually here; it receives separate critical discussion later, in Section 3.2. Her name, like her husband's, is not given until further on in the story. In the Tale it is spelled indifferently Alison or Alisoun, for metre, rhyme or euphony; this variation is not maintained in the present study, where Alisoun is preferred. (Nicholas also appears as Nicholay, and Absolon as Absolom.) Though much is said about Alisoun's body, the description dwells more on her clothes; the suggestiveness of her clothing, together with some lip-smacking comments by the Miller on her disposition, enhance the attractiveness of her evident sexual presence. Mediaeval people listened to many sermons against the sinfulness of dressing to attract men.

The clinch (lines 163-98)
With a mock-deferential bow to the audience, reminding us of the

supposedly oral delivery of the tale, the Miller wastes no time in getting the young lovers together. Nicholas's approach could not be more direct: 'and privately he caught her by the cunt' (line 168). The word *queynte* was evidently not so firmly barred from ordinary usage as it has been for the last three hundred years. Andrew Marvell made a similar play on 'quaint' in his famous poem 'To His Coy Mistress' three hundred years after Chaucer, but since then its literary use has until recently been unimaginable outside pornography. Despite his efforts in *Lady Chatterley's Lover*, written in1926-7 but not published in Britain until 1961, D. H. Lawrence did not succeed in restoring it to use. It was an improper if not an obscene word in Chaucer's day. In the couplet in which it occurs it comes as a comical anticlimax. The rhyming of words of identical sound but different senses – known in French as *rime riche* – was appreciated in the verse of the time: the first line of the couplet could be translated 'For students are very subtle and very ingenious' (that is, clever in making logical distinctions); the contrast between *queynte* as 'curious, speculative, *recherché*' and its other meaning is clearly meant to evoke a laugh. *Hende* Nicholas is clever with his hands. Laughter would continue at the would-be fashionable love-talk with which he accompanies his basic approach. Nicholas was introduced in line 92 as an expert on *deerne love* (secret passion) of the sort that had long been fashionable at Court, but expert also in *solas* – the sweet reward of such love. In the *Knight's Tale*, Palamon and Arcite had languished for years, without Emelye even being aware of their existence, let alone their passion. But Nicholas's secrecy is expedient rather than noble. He has none of the sense of his own unworthiness nor of his lady's honour which are the essence of the courtly lover's code. He calls her his *lemman* (sweetheart, darling), which is less than adoring, but he claims, like the lover in a courtly romance, that he will die – if she does not let him 'have his will'. As his will is pressingly physical, the request is less noble than the courtier's usual plea that the lady should hear his suit; but Alisoun is not a lady. Chaucer's humour here combines the Miller's mockery of the Knight's idea of love with courtly amusement at how small-town folk ape their betters. The parody of 'courtly love' is to be a more prominent feature in the character of Absolon.

Alisoun's animal reaction is likened to that of a colt put into a shoeing frame. She has already been likened to a weasel, a playful kid or calf, and an excitable colt. She struggles to escape, threatening to cry out, but Nicholas does not take his hands away and she is persuaded to 'grant him her love'; a phrase the effect of which is lowered by the addition of 'atte laste', when the seduction can only have lasted a few minutes. She swears by the saint towards whose shrine the Miller is riding that she will deceive her husband with Nicholas as soon as she gets the chance. Nicholas sees no difficulty in conning a carpenter, and they part after further exciting preliminary love-making. The strumming of the little harp in which Nicholas then indulges seems to give a sexual association to music in the *Miller's Tale*.

Absolon (lines 199–243)

At this point we apparently depart from the broad high-road of the *fabliau* plot and a new character is introduced, the parish clerk Absolon. Alisoun, having piously promised adultery, now goes to church on the holy day to do 'Christ's own work' – that is, *opus dei*, divine service; or rather to show off her gleaming forehead, which she has washed after doing her housework so that it will attract admiration. A high forehead was fashionable but should have been covered in church. Sermons against female vanity often mention attire in church, where women could be observed by men.

Absolon's portrait is a set piece, the niceties of which are given discussion in Chapter 5. Absolon was a familiar figure from the Bible (2 Samuel 18) in sermons and church paintings and windows, famous for his long golden hair as an example of masculine vanity. Chaucer used him as a type of beauty in his famous short poem 'Hide, Absolon, thy gilte tresses clere' (thy shining golden tresses). He rebelled against his father, King David, and in escaping from a battle against David's army he rode under an oak tree in which his hair became caught, so that he was left hanging when his mule rode on, a sitting target for his enemies. Immediately after his name, Absolon's hair, in its would-be fashionable style, is elaborately described. He is a clerk in minor orders who assists at Mass, swings the thurible or censer in which incense is burned and takes the collection. He is the first of the many effeminate young curates in English literature. He is prettily dressed and fairly good at many accomplishments which the Miller would scorn as unmanly.

Absolon fancies himself as a ladies' man: he took his music into any tavern where there was a lively barmaid, and on this church holiday he ogles the ladies as he eagerly 'senses' them, not taking their church-offerings because he is too much of a gentleman. One can imagine how a comic actor would play the part. He particularly likes looking at the carpenter's sweet and sexy wife.

Absolon's wooing (lines 244–90)

Absolon's approach to the carpenter's wife is according to ideals found in books: he begs her pity, serenading her at her bedroom window by moonlight; but overlooks the fact that her husband is at home. His voice is obviously recognisable, for John asks Alisoun if she hears Absolon singing (this is the first time we hear their names). Yes, she says, perfectly. Neither of them pays any further attention, so the opening of Absolon's campaign is a flop.

Undeterred, *this joly Absolon* (an adjective nearer to French *joli* than to English *jolly*) carries on wooing day and night. This is like a courtly lover in a romance, but his broad coiffure with its lovely wide parting does not sound either elegant or manly. Still more redolent of the small-town hairdresser is his final approach: after go-betweens, declarations, warblings and aphrodisiac presents, he tries bribing her with money. The conclusion of the paragraph is masterly: it gives the great lover's thoughts on how to win the female heart. As a proverb, it is doubtless true enough, though it is already clear that Absolon is making absolutely no impression on Alisoun. But his silly little bribes do not represent *richesse*. As well as revealing Absolon's vanity and folly, this comment at the same time tells us that Alisoun has married money (John), is seduced by Nicholas's rough wooing (*strokes* in both senses) and is not interested in Absolon's *gentillesse*.

The crowning miscalculation of Absolon's wooing of Alisoun is his choice of a role in which to show off his accomplishments. In the popular mystery plays - whose contribution to the Tale is discussed in Section 3.6 - King Herod was, even more than Pilate, a ranting, raving, heavy villain. The Miller in line 16 cried out 'in Pilates voys' - a deep and drunken roar? Absolon sings in 'a loud quynyble' or counter-tenor, an artificially high male soprano voice, sung falsetto but popularly supposed to be an indication of incomplete masculinity; one may feel sure that a girl like Alisoun will share to the full any such popular misconceptions. He is, as the Miller now points out more than once, utterly wasting his time. The proverb means that the schemer on the spot makes the distant beloved seem hateful; this is the way Absolon, if he had any idea of the situation, might represent it to himself, since although Nicholas is *nye* and *hende*, and so in a position to spoil his chances with Alisoun, Absolon himself is both *ferre* and *looth*. The Miller's general analysis of the situation of the rivals reminds us once more that this is a typical set-up whose outcome is predictable. Of Alisoun's three lovers, John will be cuckolded by Nicholas, and Absolon will not get anywhere. Exactly how this will be fulfilled remains, however, unknown. The match is about to begin and we the spectators have been brought to a state of intense curiosity.

The trick (lines 291–492)

Nicholas's *wyle* to get John out of the way is fantastic and elaborate in its detail, as is the way Chaucer leads up to it, but it is simple in essence. Nicholas has identified John's weakest point, his infatuation with Alisoun; and the carpenter's ignorance and credulity offer an easy approach to this weakness. For all his mistrust of intellectuals, John implicitly believes in authority. What Nicholas tells him combines the authority of astrology and the Bible in an apparently scientific prophecy, precise in its circumstantiality: 'a Monday next, at quarter nyght'. A second Flood, like that which drowned everyone except Noah and his family, shall drown all mankind. Why should Nicholas have chosen this device? Because in the mystery plays, which enacted the whole of biblical history, Noah's Flood was an immensely popular episode, and John, as a carpenter, could be expected to know about Noah's Flood. For the guild – trade-association – of the carpenters had the responsibility of building a stage Ark for the play of Noah's Flood. An extra twist is that this carpenter is extremely hazy about Noah's Flood: he claims to have heard about it a very long time ago, but refers to Noah as 'Nowel' (that is, Noel, Christmas). Despite this he is so gullible that he still swallows Nicholas's absurd story.

The lead-up to the confidence-trick reminds us that the young pair are equally keen on cheating the *sely* man under whose roof they sleep: 'For this was his desir and hire also'. Nicholas tells Alisoun exactly what to say, a plausible speech which you can hear her saying, even in its indirect form. Nicholas stays in his room all Saturday and Sunday. Then at last John opens his mouth and, as so often in Chaucer, a stock figure leaps into life. If the reader had encountered John the Carpenter at some later stage of literary history – say, in a Shakespearian comedy or a novel by Henry Fielding – he would seem a familiar type, springing from a long stage tradition. Perhaps Chaucer drew on the mystery plays not only for the allusions to them which abound in the *Miller's Tale* but also for their live tradition of characterisation. As it is, John is an astonishingly vivid character: gnarled, impenetrably stupid, practical, self-important, naïve, superstitious, full of platitudes, kindly enough, a small-town Polonius without guile. He is not just a crabbed, jealous old husband. With his introduction the whole story gains a peasant breadth and solidity. All his idioms are immediately provincial, colloquial and next-door: 'adrad', 'shilde', 'tikel', 'on Monday laste'. He clearly has a local accent of the sort known to stage actors as Mummerset. The element of caricature becomes unmistakable with the instruction to his servant to call at Nicholas's door or *Knokke with a stoon*.

The story also begins to move faster, with some of the manic and mechanical inevitability of a Punch and Judy show or an animated cartoon film. The servant crying and knocking like mad, the cat-hole, the moon-struck astronomer, the carpenter repeatedly crossing himself – these all have the excited and frenetic simplicity of farce: people behaving like dolls on a German clock.

The introduction of the servant, apparently unnecessary, has the curious effect of making the action more comic and John's belief more plausible. The Knave's prolonged and undignified effort to get a look at Nicholas through the cat-hole 'Ful lowe upon a bord', lends urgency to his report to his master.

The carpenter's reaction to Nicholas's apparent seizure is immediately to blame it on his astrology. Ignorance laughs at the downfall of learning; but to this perennial anti-intellectualism John adds the mediaeval doctrine of proper knowledge: 'Men sholde nat knowe of Goddes privetee.' The idea that God has his secrets into which man ought not to enquire may now seem obscurantist, but this ancient religious instinct lay behind the mediaeval church's condemnation of pseudo-sciences like astrology and alchemy, and colours modern attitudes to nuclear science and genetic engineering. The Miller has already invoked the notion of forbidden knowledge in line 56 of his Prologue, and linked it with over-inquisitiveness about wifely fidelity. It could be said that the Tale, like the ancient Greek myths of Oedipus or of Prometheus, shows that curiosity does not pay: John is said to keep his wife in a cage, and sends his servant to spy on Nicholas; Nicholas spies on God – neither with any ultimate success.

John claims that he had always known that Nicholas's studying would come to this: he twice calls astronomy 'astromie' – the first malapropism in English literature? – and unfortunately uses the word 'falle' three times in his head-shaking comments on the vanity of nosy astronomers. While he is orthodox in his belief that all the knowledge that is necessary to salvation is contained in the 'bileve' (the 'I believe', *Credo*), he is all the time digging a pit for himself literally to fall into. The carpenter's religion is superstitious, comically so, especially to an age with different superstitions. If he has difficulty in remembering Noah's Flood he does not know the Bible very well.

John's decency in helping his deluded young lodger expresses itself in decisive action, described with the physicality and energy which are the hallmarks of the Miller and his tale. John levers up the door (the cat-hole again?) and his knave lifts it off its hinges. Although not explicit, a huge crash is suggested by the rhythm of line 363, created by the reversed stress in the first foot. We recall that the Miller's favoured method of proving his strength was the splitting or unhinging of doors. Nicholas, in the best traditions of farce, does not move a muscle. Rapt in his vision of the end of the world, he does not stir until his by now thoroughly alarmed host has exorcised him and the room. The first stage of the trap, the gaining of John's bemused attention, has taken almost a hundred lines.

The comedy built up through these lines is of the broadest but also the most skilful sort. The narrative combines immobility on the part of Nicholas with increasingly frenzied actions and words from John, culminating in the touching outcry, 'What! Think on God, as we do, men that swinke.' The pious John is to do a great deal more hard physical work before the tale is over.

When Nicholas at last speaks, breaking out of his trance to deliver his heart-breaking message, the Tale takes on a new dimension. Even though we know that it is false, a prophecy of the end of the world is intriguing. *Eftsoones* here means 'immediately': Nicholas has been chosen as the instrument to tell mankind that it has 24 hours to live. John's aghast reaction shows implicit faith in the truth of this prophecy, but his credulity is immediately exposed by the comical rhyme of 'think', 'swink', and 'drink' and the *double entendre* of 'toucheth', which to John means 'concerneth' and to Nicholas has a more literal meaning.

First Nicholas swears John to silence by religious oaths, the terms of which are noticeable: if he tells anyone he will be *wood* (mad). John binds himself not to tell 'child ne wyf' by repeatedly swearing on Christ as Redeemer. Nicholas then announces the destruction of the world by a Flood greater than Noah's. John almost swoons at the thought of losing Alisoun.

The clerk now flatters the carpenter by taking him into his confidence. Having drunk together and shut the door, they will confer and settle the fate of mankind. With the wisdom of Solomon and the providence of Noah, the two men will save themselves (and their woman) by their superior knowledge. Nicholas lets the story out very slowly, for John's benefit, filling out his explanation with the creaking platitudes of which the carpenter is so fond, adding one or two more learned touches.

The great majority could not read and write in the Middle Ages, and there is a modern tendency to equate illiteracy with ignorance. It is sometimes imagined in countries with Protestant traditions that lay people in the Middle Ages cannot have known the Bible because they could not read Latin manuscripts. But the Church made the Bible known through the spoken word (education was entirely in clerical hands), through preaching and Bible readings in the (sung and spoken) liturgy at innumerable church attendances; not to mention the biblical stories which were depicted in stained glass and wall-paintings all over the inside of churches and in carved and painted stone on the outside of major churches. Popular religion was also disseminated outside church by the friars, not only through preaching but also through what we might now think of as cultural activity or even literature; religious songs, and more especially religious drama. The story, and the stories, of the Bible were known to the people rather than its text; although key individual texts and tags were of course current then, as now, in daily conversation, and they were often jocularly misapplied.

There are many mentions of the miracle or mystery plays in Chaucer, especially in the *Miller's Tale*, and the topic is discussed in Section 3.6. But it is clear that the carpenter ought to have known the story of Noah, so outstandingly popular and picturesque that it is still well-known through children's books and Negro spirituals to those who are ignorant of Christianity. In the Book of Genesis, after the Creation and Fall, and the stories of Cain and Abel and Adam's descendants, we come, in Genesis 6, to Noah (known in the Middle Ages as Noe, the form that his name has in the Latin Vulgate Bible that was then used). God decided to destroy mankind because of its sinfulness (often interpreted by commentators as especially referring to lechery). After the Flood only the descendants of the just man Noah and his wife survived; and God promised Noah that he would not allow mankind to be destroyed by water a second time, and gave him the rainbow as a sign of this covenant. The guild of carpenters usually had to build the Ark. If John remembers this, which is not clear, he has certainly forgotten God's promise that there will be no second Flood. He is indeed a *lewed* (ignorant) man.

The 'sorrow of Noe with his fellowship' was a standing joke in the English mystery plays. Noah has great difficulty in getting Mrs Noah into the Ark; in the Towneley Play he has to beat her. Nicholas uses this strife as an argument for three individual arks. No copulation, he sternly warns, adhering to the learned tradition that there was none in Noah's Ark.

The grave prohibition of 'sin' between John and his wife is farcical enough in the circumstances, but the shamelessness of Alisoun's pretended fidelity ('I am thy trewe, verray wedded wyf', 501) may soon pose a problem to the modern reader. We have heard John cry 'Allas, my wyf' (414), and Nicholas plays on this fear with his Disneyland fantasy of their all waking up safe on Tuesday morning, lords of the world. John's concern for his wife, after his fussing over Nicholas, may awaken our sympathies.

The execution (lines 493–548)

The confidence trick has worked and John is well and truly hooked. We may be tempted to feel sorry for him as a wronged husband who certainly loves his wife; and we are about to feel less sympathetic toward Alisoun. We are used to realistic novels and plays, in which we are invited to feel sorry for injured characters as if they were real people. John speaks so vividly that at this point we can forget that he is a caricature, although the narrator is soon to pull us back from any identifying with John's point of view.

The *fabliau* is a heartless genre, like the modern cartoon film, with rapid action and two-dimensional characters with no insides. It may be that Chaucer is slightly too realistic for the genre; it may be that mediaeval taste was harder and more robust than ours; it may be that the figure of the jealous, doting cuckold is no longer as laughable as it was, even in Latin countries with their Catholic tradition of a more forgiving attitude to sexual misconduct.

Sympathy for John may be evoked in us simply by the plot-situation, but it can scarcely survive a full response to the text, for we are constantly invited to laugh, especially at him. Nicholas calls him *wys* in 491 but the narrator immediately describes him as *sely* as he blabs the secret. Breaking a promise is always punished in stories, and we can now expect John to become *wood*. The possibility of sympathy is destroyed by the use of *privetee* and *queynte* within three lines, words which have already acquired jocular sexual meanings.

At this point, when the complete untruthfulness of Alisoun is revealed, and the extent of John's impending humiliation can be guessed - a point when a whole range of audience attitudes are involved as possibilities, including some cruel laughter - the narrator steps back and offers his only extended comment: it begins:

> Lo, which a greet thing is affeccioun!
> Men may dyen of imaginacioun,
> So depe may impressioun be take.

This comment must be taken as Chaucer's, not the Miller's: its head-shaking is genial, gently laughing, and, like its vocabulary, philosophical; it is, in fact, remarkably similar to several comments made by the narrator and by Theseus in the middle of the *Knight's Tale* on the folly of love. *Affeccioun* means 'feeling' not 'affectionateness'. John's wits have been, as we might say, 'affected' by his infatuation for Alisoun. The submergence of reason in emotion is now conveyed to us with wonderful precision in John's fantasy and especially in the image *walwinge as the see*. From these heights the carpenter descends into pitiable weeping and sets to work, obeying Nicholas's instructions as literally as Noe obeyed God's. The physicality of the description of the *ronges* in the ladders and the *good ale in a jubbe* are in delightful contrast with the three abstract nouns in the lines beginning the paragraph.

This materiality of description, packed with detail yet economical, continues until John, weary of business but having said his prayers, falls asleep, and snores – *for his heed mislay* – and the lovers speed off to his bed. Their loving is described lightly and indirectly: 'revel', 'melodie', 'bisynesse of mirthe and of solas'. There is none of the Miller's own coarseness, no lip-smacking detail, and no condemnation. Indulgence is extended as if to an innocent jape. But the joyful moment is preceded by the lovers' silent efficiency in getting 'there as the carpenter is wont to lie'. And the moment slides, by a skilful transition, into a different kind of time:

> Til that the belle of laudes gan to ringe,
> And freres in the chauncel gonne singe.

The immediate plot-purpose of the transition is to bring us to Absolon. But the world of 'melody' and 'the business of mirth' modulates into the world of antiphonal singing of the praise of God in the cool chancel at dawn, a reminder of other joys and other harmonies; by the light of which it is difficult to forget altogether that Nicholas is engaged in adultery in his landlord's bed with his landlord's 'trewe, verray wedded wyf'. It is typical of Chaucer's light touch to remind us of the non-temporal by telling us the time.

Absolon's kiss (lines 549–633)

It is a puzzle why the monk draws the *amorous* Absolon apart out of the church, unless he is reflecting the marked discreetness of the parish clerk's chance enquiry about John. If so, it suggests that a worldly conspiratorial discretion was normal among Absolon's clerical acquaintance. This quiet little scene adds further to the detailed realism of the tale's social setting.

Now that the coast is clear, the great lover plans his next move: he will sleep in the daytime so that he will be fresh at cock-crow to beg for the kiss which, his itching mouth tells him, Alisoun will certainly let him have. He has dreamed of oral satisfaction, and his preparations are concentrated on sweetening his mouth and combing his hair. The height of the window above the ground is again established before Absolon announces his presence in a ladylike manner.

His prepared speech is a tissue of echoes from the Song of Songs, as illustrated in Section 3.5. But even without any awareness on our part of parody or misapplication, it is clear that Absolon has, from Alisoun's point of view, got it all wrong again. Even if she had been alone, she could never have been interested in the love-sick maid of the last line. Absolon apes the humble approach of the chivalrous lover, but he feels too sorry for himself to convey any feelings of adoration. He presents himself as a whimpering lamb desperate for the teat. The bleating lamb and the moaning dove suggests how boring to the sexually mature is the sound of a self-pitying adolescent lover. For a fastidious youth he is curiously distasteful in his images of himself sweating and sweltering. The speech is designed to make the kind of kiss it earns seem horribly appropriate.

Alisoun's contemptuous verbal reaction is certainly understandable, though the middle lines of her retort ('I love another') are a reminder to the audience of whom, 'by Jhesu', this other ought to have been. Absolon will not take a warning and, with a ridiculous pathos, demands at least a kiss.

The economy of the climax leaves little to the critic but to exclaim in admiration. It must be said that in his vanity Absolon does everything he can to make the situation worse. He kneels (like a lamb), thinks himself a lord, hopes for more, and wipes his mouth. His essential innocence, and the peculiarly painful nature of his silliness and of his humiliation, is revealed in his reaction. He 'thought it was amis,/For wel he wiste a woman hath no berd'. (He must have said something to this effect, for Nicholas repeats it.) The line giving the comment of Alisoun shows that great poetry does not have to be poetic.

Revenge (lines 634–707)

On hearing Nicholas's exultant voice joining in the laughter, Absolon, no longer *jolly* but *sely* like John, sees the truth at last. He is cured of his 'maladie' of love, forswears girl-friends, and angrily vows revenge – sentiments which the Miller might approve. He remains the same, however, in his obsessive oral hygiene and his childish weeping. Delusion gives way to vengeance.

Back in the small hours of a real fourteenth-century Oxford, Gervays is at work in his smithy, and Chaucer has another of his minor conversational triumphs. Gervays heartily greets Absolon as a pursuer of girls –

the only reason he could be out in the streets, which was forbidden in the hours of darkness. The quenched spirit of Absolon now speaks in a businesslike way, and moves efficiently to his goal. His confidence trick is simple but it deceives the still exulting Nicholas, whose conceit leads him to 'amend the jape'. The rhyme of 'kisse' and 'pisse' is a warning of further anarchy and indecency.

The physical details of the final encounter are given with great clarity: 'to the haunche-bon', 'a hande-brede'. The style is at the same time effortlessly capable of expressing parody and hyperbole: Absolon's fawning request to his sweet 'bryd', Nicholas's thunder, Absolon's coolness under fire. Nicholas has overreached himself and pays the penalty. His understandable cry for water is the word John has been waiting for. Two, or three, plots have been beautifully engineered so that the word which ends two of them precipitates the end of the third.

Conclusion (lines 708–47)

The carpenter's action is on reflection slightly implausible, if not incredible for someone who has been startled out of heavy sleep. But it happens too quickly for us to disbelieve it, and we are anyway in the fantasy world of farce, where absurdity should escalate. With a final magnificent malapropism John severs the rope which holds him two floors up in the air. In practice, an audience listening to the story for the first time will have forgotten all about John and his situation. The climax of the tale is a let-down. The Miller jokes that he found no one on the way down to whom he might sell the bread and ale he had with him in his tub.

The neighbours rush from their beds at Nicholas' and Alisoun's cry for help, and come in to gawp at the concussed carpenter. He had to endure what he had brought upon himself (a broken arm). Not the least skilful aspect of the tale is how the absurdity of the story of a second Flood, which had fooled John, is now used to prove that he is mad. There actually are two kneading tubs up in the roof for folk to see; even the sceptical clerks of Oxford agree that the man is mad.

Everyone laughed at this row. The Miller ends by returning the tale to the simple truths of the *fabliau*. The carpenter's wife got laid, Absolon kissed her 'nether eye', and Nicholas got branded in the bum: God save the lot of you.

The moral

John is omitted from this final tally; but we have just heard that he had broken his arm and has been pronounced to be *wood* as a result of his humiliation. To break your arm might be serious in Chaucer's day if you were old, and it might put an end to John's carpentry. To treat the story realistically is clearly inappropriate – we are not meant to speculate on whether John continues to let a room out to Nicholas, but rather to see John's injury as morally parallel to those of Nicholas and Absolon. Each has been punished in the part wherein he offended, as mediaeval law often demanded. If a fishmonger in the City of London was convicted of selling rotten fish he was placed on his horse facing backwards and had to endure a ride through the City with rotten fish strapped to his nose: making the punishment fit the crime. In Islamic law the punishment for theft is to have your hand cut off. Absolon has too oral a view of sex, while Nicholas's is too basic; their punishments fit their crimes.

Alisoun, however, has merely been *swyved*, which was what she wanted, and she seems to have enjoyed it. She escapes the retaliatory scheme of justice in the tale. Perhaps in such cases women – rather irrational creatures according to the moral theologians of the day – might not be considered as moral agents; certainly in the *plot* of the tale Alisoun, like Emelye in the *Knight's Tale*, is the prize, the quarry, the cause and end of the action, and not primarily an agent.

Should we expect justice from a folk-tale? Yes, a rough but moral justice is exactly what they impose on the unfairness of life. Should we expect justice from the dishonest Miller? His tale shows a Darwinian survival of the fittest: in nature, old men should not 'keep' young mates, and the cunning Nicholas is a fitter mate for the wild young Alisoun. We may be sure that the Miller enjoys the humiliation of the effeminate Absolon. But should we expect justice from Chaucer? Surely we should, although in the balancing of the *Canterbury Tales* as a whole rather than in every tale. Chaucer tells us in the last line of the *Miller's Prologue* that 'men shal nat maken ernest of game'. The *Miller's Tale* is clearly *game*, a jest; a fantasy full of anarchy, indecency, folly, farce and laughter. The carnival spirit should not be reduced into propriety. Laughter may eventually be compatible, however, with a theological understanding of life.

The morality of the tale attaches to the three lovers of Alisoun, each of whom is punished. In the eyes of the Church as well as of Nicholas, rich and impotent old men should not purchase the exclusive rights to attractive young women. The three purposes of marriage in traditional Catholic teaching are the procreation of human beings, the avoidance of sexual sin, and the mutual solace and comfort of the partners. None of these aims is met by such a marriage.

In consequence, John's punishment is more severe and long-lasting than those of the youngsters. Nicholas is punished for his intellectual conceit and the low ends to which he devotes it; Absolon has his girlish fantasies and his excessive fastidiousness exploded by two outrageous insults to them: short, sharp shocks which will do the clerks good. There is thus a crude morality in the tale which at points coincides with certain 'Darwinian' instincts of the Miller; with folk-tale fantasy; and even with Christian teaching about marriage. But this scheme excludes Alisoun, and excludes also an amoral joy in fantasies of chaos, absurdity, indecency, slapstick and cruelty. The justice of the tale is more aesthetic than ethical: the three men are all neatly punished for their vanity. Alisoun seems to have the last laugh; but we have seen her descend to a very low level of morality and indignity, exhibiting to Absolon what it is that makes her attractive. The tale could certainly be described as a comedy of human vanity: the last thing we hear is the superior laughter of the Oxford clerks.

3 THEME AND SIGNIFICANCE

The *Miller's Tale* is a sexual comedy, in which the attractions of a young woman cause physical injury to her husband and her lover and humiliation to another suitor. It shows how love blinds men to their own folly and how pride comes before a fall. Sexual vanity takes the form of uxoriousness (excessive devotion to a spouse) in John; intellectual conceit in Nicholas; and narcissism in Absolon.

The above is a very abstract summary of the Tale, which might appeal to a practical Christian moralist of Chaucer's day. To describe the *Miller's Tale* as moral perhaps seems a sophisticated attempt to wrench the facts. After all, it is a dirty joke, a Millerish revenge on the Knight and an attack on the Reeve, with no high motives. Why attempt to rescue the Tale for Christianity?

The world in which Chaucer lived and wrote was so permeated with Christian values that there was no non-Christian art. Even villains like the Miller and opportunists like his four main characters worked (sinfully enough) within Christian categories because the air they breathed was Christian. Thus the Miller's mockery of 'courtly love' is in terms of a Christian realism, and his elaborate dirty joke is made by Chaucer constantly to invoke biblical parallels because these were the chief parallels available. Even the Reeve's Tale, which has no biblical archetypes behind it and no allusions to the Annunciation, could be described as Christian bawdy. The plots themselves are universal and non-Christian, based on the sexual envy and revenge of the young upon the old, but a tale is more than its plot. In the Tale, only Nicholas knows his love for Alisoun for what it is: John and Absolon both idolise her. A Christian moralist would approve of their punishments, and certainly of Nicholas's, as poetic justice; without approving of the motives of the three punishers.

3.1 BAWDY

The bawdy element itself, however embarrassing, deserves discussion, as it is the kernel of the folk-tale which became a *fabliau*, which in its turn became Chaucer's *Miller's Tale*. Bawdy comes from 'bawd', a procurer of prostitutes; hence an adjective and noun for dirty talk: Chaucer tells us that the Miller was 'a janglere and a goliardeys/And that was moost of sinne and harlotries'. There is no *harlotrie* in the narrow sense in the *Miller's Tale*, but there is a lot of obscenity. The action of the tale involves not only sexual immorality in the form of physical seduction and adultery, but also an extreme indecency in the form of arse-kissing and arse-branding. The actual adultery is dealt with rapidly and modestly enough (*revel* and *melodie, mirth* and *solas*) but the bum-out-of-the-window material is given epic treatment. Not only is it conceived and executed with a Peeping Tom's glee and detail, it is painfully explicit. Absolon kisses 'full savourly' . . . 'a thing al rough and long y-herd'; little is left to the imagination. Of course, the incident is fantastic: it is not probable that in the history of the human race anyone has kissed any one else's arse under the romantic impression that they were about to kiss them on the lips. But if they were to do so, this is what it would be like.

'Kiss my arse' is a proverbial expression of contempt, and the Miller shares the feeling of Alisoun and Nicholas that this is what is called for by the affectation of Absolon that love is nothing but sweetness and kisses, and that its physicality can be refined and perfumed out of existence. But the moral aspect of the punishment, or cure, of Absolon, is secondary to its comic function. It is certainly very funny; although, as always, it is not easy to say exactly why we laugh. Our laughter is not just appreciative of Chaucer's skill. In what happens to Absolon our own finer feelings are vicariously violated, and we recognise the anarchic nature of our own sexual appetite and imagination when we have our noses rubbed in the actuality. The suddenness of the shock is comical, yet it also fuels our enjoyment of Absolon's revenge on his tormentors. The Greek philosopher of the fourth century BC, Aristotle, whose *Poetics* have so influenced modern criticism, taught that the experience of Tragedy purged (by *catharsis*) the emotions of pity and terror. Notes on his lectures on Comedy are scrappy; but in the various explosions, screams, breakages and hoots of laughter at the end of the *Miller's Tale* there may also be a comic 'cathartic' effect on the audience.

There has been a tendency in modern criticism to minimise the indecency of Chaucer. This is as bad as making too much of it, as the eighteenth century did. John Dryden and Alexander Pope appreciated Chaucer as (among other things) a bawdy jester; and, on Boxing Day 1801, Dorothy Wordsworth records that she read her brother William the *Miller's Tale*; but in the nineteenth century bawdy became unacceptable and eventually unmentionable. Matthew Arnold thought Chaucer lacked 'high seriousness'. In the modern reaction to Victorian prudery, there was an effort to reclaim Chaucer's 'low' bawdy, but at the cost of overlooking its often 'high' tone. In general, Chaucer has been seen by English critics as a humorous and gentle writer, humane and indulgent of human weakness, if orthodox in his final Christian attitudes; his bawdy is bright, sane fun, light in spirit, and certainly free from any titillating tendency to deprave or corrupt. The *Miller's Tale* bears this out. But the tales of the Reeve, Cook, Merchant and Shipman are harsher and less gentle, and there is an edge and a point to the obscene elements in the tale of the Summoner, the epilogue of the Pardoner and the prologue of the Wife of Bath.

If the *Miller's Tale* is read as a quick and external record of a farcical action, it is funny and good fun; and it must surely remain both after a more fully comprehending reading. But the essential obscenity of the tale's climax is in no way reduced by an appreciation of the outrageous stream of puns, nudges and jokes with which the Miller regales us. We have noted the puns on 'hende', and 'queynte' (the 'thing which toucheth me and thee' of line 386), and the care with which Absolon's obsessions are detailed before their destruction. There is also a general indecent suggestivity about 'privete', *compaignie*, Nicholas's musical instrument, the cat-hole, the 'saving' of John's wife, and much more. Not to mention the crudity of the animal functions on which the tale turns. This is frank and simple – 'good clean dirt' – characteristic of a face-to-face farmyard society. But the many biblical parallels certainly involve a blasphemy which greatly intensifies the shocking inversion of proper sexual and human relations – making the tale funnier but also more obscene and harsher. If this dimension is appreciated, it becomes much harder to sentimentalise or idealise Alisoun.

3.2 ATTITUDES TO WOMEN: ALISOUN

After the masculine world of early medieval literature, the sudden literary upsurge of interest in women in the twelfth century and afterwards is one of the most striking phenomena in the history of western culture. The Knight gets off his horse and passes the time of day with a shepherdess. The cult of the Virgin Mary is paralleled by the cult of the lady in the poetry of the troubadours. And much literature, both lyric and romance, is written to and for women, though not often by them. Alisoun's portrait (lines 125–62) is celebrated for several reasons. She is the first attractive young woman described in any detail in English literature, though there are many heroines of a more conventional sort in earlier romances. This has caused some modern (male) critics to lose their heads.

Why the impressionability of some modern critics? They were disposed to welcome the fact that, in this pre-modern period, relations between the sexes had at last become an important subject in European literature, a literature increasingly secular and vernacular. And the mode of treatment of all subjects including the human figure, began to admit a kind of realism alongside allegory. Realism and three-dimensionality have, since the Renaissance, been prized, both in art and in fiction, and we have come to expect them. So the portrait of Alisoun has come to be read realistically. And since her physical attractions are not described with any evident disapproval, but on the contrary with warmth and enthusiasm (due in part to the Miller), she has been seen as a naturally attractive creature whose sexual appeal is innocent. If her later behaviour shows she is no better than she should be, well (so the argument goes) that is scarcely her fault. A particular recommendation of Alisoun's to this school of thought is that her description is full of comparisons with innocent, natural things: morning milk, the early pear-tree in blossom, sheep's wool, the swallow. In particular:

> Thereto she coude skippe and make game,
> As any kide or calf folwinge his dame.   *its*
> Her mouth was sweete as bragot or the meeth,   *mead*
> Or hoord of apples leyd in hey or heeth.   *heather*
> (151–4)

These lines seem to set the seal of innocence on her powerful natural appeal. They also summon up a modern nostalgia for a legendary Merrie England, where life was simpler, innocent and more fun, and apples tasted better. Shakespeare's Sir Toby Belch speaks for this nostalgia when he says to the Puritan Malvolio in *Twelfth Night*: 'Dost thou think, because thou art virtuous, there shall be no more cakes and ale?' The English Protestant Reformation of the second quarter of the sixteenth century established a different set of social ideals: a married clergy, a more sober style of manners and dress, a respect for thrift and propriety, a dislike of public merry making except on state occasions, a suppression of popular religious feasts. It is certain that the Reformation suppressed some country merrymaking, along with the monasteries and the Mystery Plays, and introduced a more censorious public attitude to sexual misconduct. Even without any such vision of a Merrie England, the sensuous evocation of line 154 is magically fetching.

But we have seen reason to believe that everything about Alisoun is calculated by Chaucer to appeal. Her mouth especially is appealing to Absolon; who wishes to kiss it with a fervour that apes that of the Song of Songs. To concentrate on the innocence of nature in Alisoun's description is to ignore the first and last of her comparisons: her body is first of all compared to the devious, sexy weasel; and she is lastly a primrose or another flower known as the pigs-eye. This introduces the Miller's final tribute: she would be a good lay for a lord, or a good wife for a yeoman (a superior servant).

To her animal qualities of skittish liveliness she adds a wanton eye, and eye-catching and revealing clothes. She even plucks her eyebrows, then a clear sign of coquetry and artificiality, except at Court. The key to her conception lies in line 145: she was the most attractive wench imaginable; or rather, her sexual allure *exceeded* any man's imagination. This ought to make it clear that Alisoun is essentially a literary type, not an individual, a type that owes its power to the imagination of the opposite sex, and therefore combines some apparent innocence with much promise of exciting experience.

This point has been laboured because some readers are taken in by the allure of the portrait. Any illusion that Alisoun is a nice girl could not survive an intelligent reading of her response to Nicholas's assault. It becomes clear, as soon as she opens her mouth, that her attractions, though irresistible, are entirely physical. The vulgarity of her conversation is exceeded only by the shamelessness of her conduct. In a heartless way, it is all very amusing, merry and excusable, but it was never meant to be wholesome.

The moral of the *Miller's Tale*, at a natural level, is that a jealous old husband will not succeed in keeping for himself a wild young animal *narwe in cage* (line 116), especially if there is a young man already inside the cage. From a supernatural point of view it has the same realistic moral, but the antics, though just as comic, are not so humorous. Later in the *Tales*, the *Prioress's Prologue* is a hymn to the Virgin, the same Virgin of Nicholas's song *Angelus ad virginem*. It contains the lines:

> O mooder Mayde! o mayde Mooder free!
> O bush unbrent, brennynge in Moyses sighte,

> That ravyshedest doun fro the Deitee
> Thurgh thyn humblesse, the Goost that in th'alighte. . .
>
> (467–70)

The attractive humility which led to Mary's being chosen puts Alisoun into a different perspective.

3.3 *THE KNIGHT'S TALE*

The Miller has promised to *quite*, answer, the Knight's noble tale, and he carries out his claim. To understand the *Miller's Tale*, it is an advantage as well as a pleasure to have read the *Knight's Tale*: it inspires several things in the *Miller's Tale*, chief of which is a pair of courtly lovers, who provide a role-model for Absolon. The *Miller's Tale* is a detailed parody or burlesque of the Knight's, designed to refute its pretensions. This is therefore the point at which to offer a *resumé* of the *Knight's Tale*, without stressing unduly those features which re-appear in the Miller's distorting mirror.

The story is a romance set in ancient Greece. Two young cousins, Palamon and Arcite, are rivals in love for Emelye, whom they have seen through the window of their prison. They are Theban prisoners at the court of Theseus, Duke of Athens; she is the queen's young sister, and is quite ignorant of their love. Arcite is released and banished: he returns to Athens in disguise, but is unable to declare his love. When Palamon escapes, the cousins meet and fight. Theseus discovers them fighting and condemns them to death; but, relenting, he announces that a tournament will be held in a year and a day from then to settle the issue. Arcite wins the tournament but is thrown from his horse at the moment of triumph and dies. Palamon, who is supported by Venus, survives, and, after lavish mourning for Arcite, Theseus gives Emelye's hand to Palamon in marriage.

Detailed summary

Part I

Duke Theseus, having conquered the Amazons and married their queen, Ypolita, brings her and her sister Emelye home to Athens. He is met at the gate by the weeping widows of those who had fought against Creon, tyrant of Thebes: they complain that Creon will not allow their husbands' bodies to be buried, and throw themselves on the mercy of Theseus. Theseus kills Creon in battle.

Among the bodies of the dead are found, still alive, the young Theban cousins Arcite and Palamon. Taken back to Athens, they are put in prison. One May morning, through the window, they see Emelye in the garden, fall in love with her and begin to quarrel over who saw her first. Later, at the request of their mutual friend Perotheus, Theseus releases Arcite - on the condition that Arcite should not return to Athens. Thus Arcite, though free, is banished from the sight of Emelye, and envies Palamon; while Palamon, though he can see Emelye, envies Arcite's freedom and his chance to win her hand.

Part II

The god Mercury appears to Arcite and tells him to return from Thebes to Athens. Years of the torments of love have so changed Arcite that he is able to pass unrecognised in Athens as Philostrate, a poor labourer. He is employed at the palace as a page to Emelye, and then as a squire to Theseus.

After seven years in prison, Palamon escapes and hides in a wood near Athens. Next morning he hears Arcite, who has risen to do observance to May, lamenting his hopeless situation. Palamon challenges Arcite to the death for the hand of Emelye. Arcite provides Palamon with food, bedding and arms, and next morning they fight. Theseus, out hunting, comes upon his young enemies fighting, and condemns them to death. He relents after Ypolita and Emelye have asked for mercy, and appoints that in a year and a day the lovers, each supported by one hundred knights, shall fight a formal combat for the hand of Emelye.

Part III

Theseus builds a theatre for the lists, with three temples, one for Venus, one for Mars and one for Diana - respectively the deities of love, war and chastity. Palamon and Arcite return, each with his hundred knights, led respectively by Lygurge of Trace and Emetreus of Ind. All are well entertained by Theseus. On the night before the tournament, Palamon goes to the temple of Venus, and prays that the goddess will give him his love. The statue gives a sign that, after a delay, his boon will be granted. Emelye prays to remain a maid; or if she has to have one of them, that it may be him that desires her most. After an obscure omen, Diana declares that Emelye must wed. Mars grants Arcite's request, which is for victory. There is strife in heaven between Venus and Mars;

Saturn, here the god of devious misfortune, promises Venus that Palamon shall have his lady.

Part IV
Theseus restricts the use of killing weapons, and turns the battle into a tournament. At the end of the day it is Palamon who is overpowered and dragged to the stake of the other party. Theseus proclaims that Arcite shall have Emelye. But Saturn arranges that, as Arcite rides towards Emelye, his horse stumbles and he is thrown to the ground. His injuries eventually prove fatal; in his dying speech he commends Palamon to Emelye. Amid universal grief, Theseus is comforted by his father, Egeus. He builds a tomb for Arcite in the grove where the two lovers had fought, and provides an elaborate funeral. Years later Theseus sends for Palamon and Emelye and after a philosophical speech advises them to stop mourning and get married, which they do, and live happily ever after.

3.4 PARODY

The basic similarity between the *Knight's* and *Miller's Tales* lies in the triangular situation of two young men in love with the same girl, one (Palamon/Absolon) more infatuated and less practical than the other (Nicholas/Arcite). Emelye and Alisoun are, of course, opposites, but each represents the ideal love-object for her level of society. She is in each case in the control of a much older man, though Theseus is Emelye's 'guardian' whereas John is Alisoun's husband, and wise rather than foolish. The similarity between the tales thus often takes the form of contrast. But since the plots of most stories can be simplified until they look similar, is it perhaps a mistake to take so literally the Miller's boast that he will *quit* the Knight's tale? The *Reeve's Tale*, for example, which has nothing to do with the *Knight's*, also has two young men wronging an older husband.

The clinching parallel comes early, with line 18 of the *Tale* itself: *Allone, withouten any compaignye*. This line is the climax to Arcite's dying speech, itself the climax of the *Knight's Tale*, in which the victor of the tournament, whom Emelye has begun already to prefer, has the prize snatched from his grasp, and addresses a farewell to the girl who has never known him, whom he has worshipped and suffered for from afar. It is a great pathetic speech, tugging at the heart-strings like an *aria* in Italian opera. Here is the central passage in Arcite's speech:

> Allas, the wo! allas, the peynes stronge,
> That I for yow have suffred, and so longe!
> Allas, the deeth! allas, myn Emelye!
> Allas, departynge of our compaignye!
> Allas, my hertes queene! *allas, my wyf*!
> Myn hertes lady, endere of my lyf!
> What is this world? what asketh men to have?
> Now with his love, now in his colde grave
> *Allone, withouten any compaignye.*
>
> (my italics; lines 2771-79)

The Miller introduces Nicholas as an accomplished and discreet lover
who looks as meek as a maiden; the word *sweet* occurs four times in his
portrait. But immediately after this introduction of the *riche gnof*'s
lodger as a clerk, astrologer, and lover whose virginal looks help him in
the discreet pursuit of love, the Miller tells us:

> A chambre hadde he in that hostelrye
> Allone, withouten any compaignye. . . .
>
> (95-6)

The implication, especially after the Miller has announced that he will
tell how a clerk cuckolds a carpenter, is that the occupant of this
chambre will not lack *compaignye* for long. This line mocks the pathos
of its original context and proclaims that the *Miller's* is to be a parody
of the *Knight's Tale*, and a detailed parody. Another echo of Arcite's
farewell: John's first words when hearing from his astrological lodger
that mankind is to be drowned are: 'Allas, my wyf!' The main points of
this parody derive from the rivalry of the love-triangle. The three arks
that John places in the roof are like the three temples Theseus builds to
Mars, Venus, and Diana for Arcite, Palamon and Emelye. The encounter
between Nicholas and Absolon at John's window is a burlesque version
of the tournament. The Miller's astrology replaces the Knight's pagan
gods. And the Oxford clerks' final laughter replaces the mourning of
the women of Athens.

Even in summary, the chivalry and ceremony of the *Knight's Tale*
make the *Miller's* seem short and quick. In the Miller's view, actions
speak louder than words, and lovers should come to the point. He
would have agreed with Donne when, two hundred years later, he wrote
in 'Love's Progress':

> Whoever loves, if he do not propose

The right true end of love, he's one who goes
To sea for nothing but to make him sick.

Accordingly the hands of Nicholas are more effective in winning Alisoun than the words of Absolon. But the *plot* of the *Miller's Tale* has almost as much action in it as does the Knight's. The difference in length is due to the fullness with which the Knight describes the noble life. However, the *Miller's Tale* is very much richer in detail than the usual *fabliau*. Several of the *fabliaux* in Boccaccio's *Decameron* are only a couple of pages long. Chaucer, however, found little to interest him in a mere dirty joke, and, as often in the *Canterbury Tales*, has enriched the basic story with a quantity and quality of detail which transform it into a work of the highest, as well as the lowest, interest.

The *Miller's Tale* is a parody not only of the *Knight's*, but also of romance conventions in general. Nicholas is *hende* (a stock epithet for the hero in popular romances, meaning 'gracious'); Absolon has *eyen greye as goos*, like a romance heroine, and his conduct of the wooing is a comic misapplication of the code of the courtly lover. This is well demonstrated by the critic E. Talbot Donaldson in an essay on 'The *Miller's Tale* and the Language of Popular Romance'. It is clearly to the Miller's purpose to mock any idealisation of love, in the *Knight's Tale* and in life itself. Love, in his view, is sex misunderstood.

3.5 BIBLICAL PARODY

The animalism of the Miller's own nature shows up in many details of the description of Alisoun and of Absolon's humiliation. It also comes into Absolon's declaration of love: 'What do ye, hony comb, sweete Alisoun', where he describes himself sweating and sweltering like a lamb after the teat. But this speech is also a parody not of the terms of a 'courtly love' speech, but full of travestied echoes of the Song of Songs (also known as The Song of Solomon, The Canticle of Canticles, and Canticles), the passionate Old Testament love-song, interpreted mystically as a celebration of the union of Christ and his bride, the Church. I reproduce (with my italics) the relevant verses from the Douay version of the Bible, which is made from the Latin Vulgate used in Chaucer's day: 'Let him *kiss me* with the kiss of his mouth: for thy breasts are better than wine, smelling sweet of the best ointments' (1.1-2); 'The voice of my beloved, behold he cometh leaping upon the mountains, skipping over the hills. My beloved is like a roe, or a young hart. Behold he *standeth* behind *our wall*, looking through the *windows*, looking through the lattices. Behold, my beloved *speaketh to me*: Arise, make haste, my love, my dove, my beautiful one, and come' (2.8-10); 'The voice of the *turtle* is heard in our land' (2.12). In Chapter 4 of the Song, verses mention the cinnamon, and 'Flocks of sheep . . . all with twins'; finally, 'Thy lips, my spouse, are as a dropping *honeycomb*, *honey* and milk are *under* thy *tongue*' (4.11). The purpose of this tissue of misapplications is not to mock the biblical author, but to make Absolon, and his pretensions to love, seem even more a foolish parody of true love. The first echo from the Song of Songs comes in the initial description of Alisoun, where her breath smells like apples: 'the odour of thy [the beloved's] mouth like apples' (7.8).

It may be asked, how many of Chaucer's audience would have caught the allusion. Most would perhaps have noticed the biblical inflection without knowing the exact source. But popular knowledge of the Bible must have been better than it is in England today, as outlined earlier. Characters from the Mystery Plays are mentioned three times in the *Miller's Prologue* and *Tale*. The Miller roars like Pilate, Absolon acts the part of Herod, and Nicholas asks John about Noe's Flood; Noe then returns, twice as Noe and twice as Nowel. These can be taken as background to the *Tale*, part of the popular religion in which it is soaked. After all, two of the men are clerks (that is, clerics) and the other is a pious, not to say superstitious, carpenter who works for an Abbey. Two or three churches appear in the tale, chiefly Absolon's parish church which Alisoun attends. The narrator and the characters constantly swear by Christ and his saints, and the carpenter appropriately mentions 'Christes sweete tree'.

3.6 THE MYSTERIES

There is, however, another level of biblical allusion, reference or parody in the *Miller's Tale*, which escapes the modern eye. In the Mystery Plays, so called because they were put on by the trade guilds, known as the Mysteries (from French *métier*), there was a very well-known carpenter, Joseph. He is represented in all the English plays which survive about the Annunciation and the Nativity as a more or less comic figure.

The Mystery Plays were cycles of religious dramas which were performed in cities throughout England and Europe in the fourteenth and fifteenth centuries and were only stopped at the Reformation. They dramatised for popular audiences the story of the Bible from Creation to Doomsday. They had originated in liturgical drama inside churches, but by Chaucer's day had moved out into the secular world, where they were performed by the trade guilds in each town, in the open air on pageant wagons, especially at the feast of Corpus Christi in June. We know of cycles of plays from a score of English cities, and four cycles survive in fairly complete form, comprising scores of individual plays. Today there are quite often revivals of Nativity and Passion Plays based on the mediaeval Mysteries, and at York there have been full-scale revivals of the York Cycle. We have several plays extant in English about Noah, and about the Nativity (Herod's Massacre of the Innocents was an episode which lent itself to much violence and tears), and also about the Passion (where Pilate figures largely), so we can document the popular images to which Chaucer is appealing in his tale. Absolon, too, was a familiar biblical figure, and so was Solomon (also mentioned in the *Tale*), the supposed author of the Song of Songs. There are several surviving plays about Joseph, but he is not mentioned in the *Tale*.

However, the Miller announces that he will tell 'a legend and a lyf/ Both of a carpenter and of his wyf'. A *legend* is usually a saint's life. The tale begins with 'a riche gnof that geestes held to bord,/And of his craft he was a carpenter./This carpenter had wedded newe a wyf. . .'. The poor scholar he lodges is 'lyk a maiden meke for to se'; he makes 'melodie' on his psaltery at night: 'And *Angelus ad virginem* he soong'. This hymn or song on the Annunciation survives to this day; it has a delightful tune, and tells how the angel Gabriel came into the Virgin Mary's locked room to tell her that she was to be the mother of Jesus. Nicholas is no angel, and Alisoun no virgin; but John, like Joseph, is a carpenter.

In the New Testament, Joseph is an upright man: 'When as his mother Mary was espoused to Joseph, before they came together, she was found with child, of the Holy Ghost. Whereupon Joseph her husband, being a just man, and not willing publicly to expose her, was minded to put her away privately. But while he thought on these things, behold an Angel of the Lord appeared to him in his sleep, saying: Joseph, son of David, fear not to take unto thee Mary thy wife, for that which is conceived in her is of the Holy Ghost' (Matthew 1. 18-20). In the next chapter Herod threatens the child and Joseph is warned by an angel to take Mary and Jesus into Egypt; after Herod's death, an angel tells Joseph to go back to Israel and another message tells him to go into Galilee. In the canonical Gospel, then, Joseph is already trusting and prone to angelic visitations. In the Apocrypha he is not only old but stupid; in the Mysteries he has degenerated into a comic, rustic, jealous husband, suspicious of his wife's virtue.

It seems clear that there is a persistent reflection of the Annunciation in early scenes of the *Miller's Tale*, though in inverted form. The similarities are greater with Absolon than with Nicholas, whose salutation is unlike the angel's, though Alisoun's reply is a kind of *Fiat* (Mary's acceptance: 'Be it done unto me according to thy word'). Absolon looks like an angel in a mediaeval painting:

> Crul was his heer, and as the gold it shoon,
> And strouted as a fanne large and broode.

He wears a 'gay surplys/As whit as is the blosme upon the rys'. These are angelic, and so are his kneeling at the bedroom window, his last words to her ('lemman, thy grace'), and his *gittern*. It is true that Absolon is much more obviously a travesty of the courtly lover serenading his lady, and the properties singled out here are primarily secular satire. But the tale is so full of popular religion (the references to Herod and Nowel remind us of Christmas) that a reference to the original eternal triangle is always latent. Many of the parallels are pictorial: Absolon kneels thrice at the bower window, in a *tableau* not unlike a typical late-mediaeval Annunciation, where Gabriel is reverent, lower than Mary and framed outside the bedroom. Absolon is also a singer and an incense-swinger, like the angels in mediaeval pictures of heaven. The 'melodie' in John's bed reminds us of this. It lasts 'Til that the belle of laudes gan to ringe,/And freres in the chauncel gonne singe'. In the illustrated mediaeval prayer-books known as the Books of Hours (after the Hours of the Divine Office) the Annunciation is always portrayed at Matins. Matins and Lauds, the 'night hours' of the Office, were sung together before dawn. The miniature of the Annunciation always appears above the words: *Domine labia mea aperies/Et os meum annunciabit laude tuam* (Lord, thou openest my lips, and my mouth shall announce thy praise).

In mediaeval art, the sexuality of the Annunciation is sublimated – for Gabriel is a being without sex, and Mary a virgin – but it is nevertheless real: a spiritual sexuality is depicted by many mediaeval artists in the Virgin's shy recoil from and acceptance of the Angel's greeting. The references to the sexuality of the Annunciation made in the *Miller's Tale* go beyond literary parody to render the antics in the *Tale* not only anarchic and indecent but obscene. The extended use of blasphemy (still common in Latin Catholic countries) is unfamiliar and somewhat shocking to us. The effect of it is to reinforce the burlesque element in the *Tale*, to make it harsher and at the same time sillier. The lowness and silliness of human vanity and lust seem all the greater and more impenetrable against the simple *Fiat* of Mary at the Annunciation, a subject which finds mediaeval song-writers and artists at their most lyrical and ravishing. One final possible biblical reference in the *Miller's Tale* is in the three tubs which John is told to put in the roof. These three arks are like the ark of the covenant in its tabernacle (Exodus 25), and so like the three tabernacles Peter wants to make at the Transfiguration (Matthew 17.4).

4 THE ART OF
THE *MILLER'S TALE*

The art of a tale lies in the telling of it, both in the narrative handling and in the language and style. Section 2.2 touched on plot, both the elegance of the double plot hanging on 'water' and also its elaboration in the tall story of the second Flood. Two further features of the narrative are narrative point of view, and realism of setting.

4.1 NARRATIVE POINT OF VIEW

Modern criticism of fiction always considers the point of view from which the story is told. In the fiction of the later twentieth century there is currently a fashion for self-conscious novelists to stress the artificiality of their fictions, and the incompleteness of our knowledge of others' motives; but popular taste still prefers the omniscience or privileged insights of the narrators of the realistic novel in the nineteenth century. The pretence on the part of the writer that he is reporting actual events and real people is still expected, and this is indeed the basis of the relationship between the writers and the readers of novels. In the work of the masters of the nineteenth-century novel, from Jane Austen to Henry James, and including French and Russian novelists, the illusion of realism is maintained: 'I am telling you a true story; I knew the people involved.'

This expectation of realism is apparently met by the Geoffrey Chaucer who tells us in the *General Prologue* of how he was at an inn in Southwark when a company of twenty-nine pilgrims arrived, how he joined them, how the Host persuaded them into a tale-telling game, and how the Knight told the first tale. The Miller's intervention makes the appearance of realism even more lively. Just as the Knight tells a knightly tale, so the Miller tells a millerish one. On the account offered here, one might well take Chaucer's story literally and attempt to believe in the Miller. Although one can hardly believe that the events in his tale really happened, one might take the nature of the tale as confirming the realism of the portrayal of the Miller's character.

But we must consider that the narrator of this tale, the Miller, is himself a creation of Chaucer. Chaucer is, in general, a tricky and joky narrator who not only makes himself out to be a very gullible pilgrim in the *General Prologue*, but also gives this pilgrim called Geoffrey Chaucer the worst tale to tell, *Sir Thopas*, a popular romance so dreadful that he is cut short in it by the Host. In revenge, the pilgrim Chaucer then tells what is perhaps the most boring tale in the collection, the *Tale of Melibee*. But the pilgrim Chaucer's first tale is a parody as well as a romance, and his second an allegory as well as a story. Little in the *Canterbury Tales* can, then, be taken merely at face value.

The question of how far we can trust the narrator arises early in the history of the English novel. Daniel Defoe's *Robinson Crusoe* (1719), a detailed fictional account of the survival of a sailor shipwrecked on a desert island, was widely believed to be true, as it purported to be. In fact, it was based upon the story of Alexander Selkirk, much amplified by Defoe's imagination. A more complex case is Jonathan Swift's *Gulliver's Travels* (1726), where Captain Lemuel Gulliver visits various countries ruled by mannikins, by giants, by intellectuals and by rational horses. Few have believed these entertaining and satirical stories, but many readers have made another assumption, that the views of Captain Gulliver, who tells the story in the first person, represent to some extent those of the author. In fact the narrator is 'a true gull', a gullible fellow, whose admiration for rational horses causes him, on his return home, to recoil from his own family with revulsion. The presumption that as a reader one should identify with the point of view of a first-person narrator has become almost second nature with many modern readers.

Mediaeval authors also seem often to rely upon this naïve impulse to identify with the 'I' who tells a story. Dante Alighieri (1265–1321) in his *Divina Commedia* tells the story of how he visited hell, purgatory and heaven. He speaks autobiographically and with a serious intensity but the story represents a movement from ignorance to understanding, and he is initially uncomprehending, almost stupid. This is true of many mediaeval 'dream-vision' poems, such as *Le Roman de la Rose*, a French poem of the thirteenth century influential in England, and also of *Pearl*, a poem by the anonymous contemporary of Chaucer who also wrote, it seems, *Sir Gawain and the Green Knight*. Like Dante, the narrator of *Pearl* is a bemused dreamer who learns painfully through his dream in which he encounters and argues with the spirit of his recently dead daughter. William Langland's *Piers Plowman* likewise takes the form of a naïve dreamer who learns from his encounters. Chaucer began his career by writing a series of dream-vision poems in which he wonderingly meets authoritative figures who enlighten him at length, usually leaving him little the wiser. The credulous pilgrim-narrator of the *Canterbury Tales* is the successor to these innocent 'I' figures, although it is clear that many of the people he meets, credible though they seem, are not to be trusted.

It is therefore evident enough that we should not necessarily trust the wisdom of the narrator of a mediaeval poem. In contrast with Dante and Langland, Chaucer embarks on his encounter with little earnestness. He is playing a game with his readers, involving them in some huge joke which is never explained – an approach which many foreigners seem to find characteristic of the English and their famous sense of humour.

Part of this game consists of increasing the verisimilitude and surface decorum of the *Tales* to a high degree of perfection. For the *Miller's Tale* is, of course, well suited to the Miller (2.2). It attacks the Knight and the Reeve, shows that cunning and violence succeed, and is full of images of splitting wood. At its beginning and end it is a typical *fabliau*, full of *harlotrie*. Its plot expresses precisely what someone such as the Miller thinks should happen to four such people as John, Nicholas, Absolon and Alisoun. Its narration has one or two touches which seem in character: 'I may not rekene hem alle' (90), and how John found no takers for his bread and ale as he fell through the air (713–4).

And yet, of course, the Miller should be too drunk to tell a tale so well. The artfulness in detail is all Chaucer's, and the larger perspectives are provided by the poet rather than by his puppet. 'Lo! which a great thing is affeccioun!' (503ff.) is Chaucer's own comment, too kindly for the Miller. It seems, then, that Chaucer is happy to disregard the dramatic proprieties, to put aside the *persona* of the Miller, and comment directly in his own person. He does so in other tales; and characters inside tales even refer to pilgrims who tell other tales. So Chaucer's respect for the conventions of narrative order and consistency is limited; at times he speaks in character, at others he reminds us that he is the author. In most of the tales he keeps well in the background, as do many of their narrators; but he is ready openly to exclaim in wonder or pity at the follies of his human creations. We have to remember that he wrote to read aloud or to be read aloud, and was used to a direct and personal communication with his audience, and ready to have a joke with them.

4.2 REALISM OF SETTING

Realism is very much a question of style. It is hard to estimate Chaucer's English and style from this distance, since the modern student ordinarily cannot compare either the language of the day, or the practice of other poets. Chaucer's English is like that of his fellow-Londoner, John Gower, smooth, rapid and up-to-date; and unlike that of Langland, a Worcestershire man, and the *Gawain*-poet, from the north-west. Both of these use the alliterative style and western dialects, which are unfamiliar and old-fashioned in comparison with London English.

As the mediaeval theory of rhetoric demanded, the style of the tale is adapted, initially at least, to its genre and its teller. As befits comedy, it is 'low', or, as we would say, colloquial, popular and racy: *gnof* at the beginning and *toute* at the end, and such touches as 'Now, sire, and eft, sire' every now and again to remind us of the churl's manner in which, as Chaucer warns us, the Miller told his tale. Decorum is maintained in the frank vulgarity of the action of the tale, heavily or lightly under-lined by the Miller at many points. Decorum is also exploited, up to the hilt, in the details of the Oxford setting: the domestic details of John's house, the three kinds of tub placed in the roof, the astrological jargon, John's superstition, the smaller sketches of the knave, the cloisterer, the smith, and the Oxford clerks, and every single conversation – all are super-realistic in the manner of the Dutch school of *genre* painting. The detailed descriptions of the hairstyles and clothing of Alisoun and Absolon are the most obvious examples of this, suggesting not just their appearance but also their social pretensions: her exposed forehead, to which she wishes to draw attention, as was fashionable among ladies of leisure, shines because it was washed so well when she had finished her *work*; and he has *Poules window corven on his shoos*. The setting is solid with this social and physical detail – with precise placing of social attitudes, and 'with bread and chese, and good ale in a jubbe'. All this is what a *fabliau* demands. The surface realism of the tale is glowingly visualised. Like Alisoun, it is appetizing, almost edible – and this glow is a tribute to Chaucer's effortless capacity as a wielder of a fresh English.

But, as we have seen earlier, only the surface of the tale is realistic. Millers do not speak in rhyming pentameters, even when drunk; and, verse-speaking aside, the elaboration and artistry of the tale is beyond any impromptu performance. This might be too obvious to mention, were it not for the persistent assumption of realism in modern commentaries. To take the opening for an example: any attempt to reproduce the Miller's drunkenness ends after twelve lines; his vocabulary would probably not have included 'Almageste', 'astrelabie' and 'augrim stones'; and the tone of these lines is too lofty and bookish:

> He knew not Catoun, for his wit was rude,
> That bad man sholde wedde his similitude.

(119-20)

Further, the tale itself is basically a fantastic farce, and the style is suitably heightened at times in order to ridicule the subject matter, by means of caricature and parody. Alisoun's allure passes man's wit to imagine, John is incredibly stupid, Nicholas is devilishly clever and Absolon painfully naïve. Obvious occasions for caricature are John's uxoriousness and superstition, Alisoun's shamelessness, and Absolon's fastidiousness. Parody is to be found throughout the tale in relation to the popular romance tradition and, in a different way, in relation to the Bible. The parody of popular romance is most easily to be seen in the portrait of Absolon, but it applies to all three young people. Nicholas is *hende*, a standard epithet for the hero of a popular romance, where it means 'gracious, noble, courtly' or merely 'nice'. Nicholas is a ruthless opportunist, who sweet-talks Alisoun at the same time as he gropes her; seduces his landlord's eighteen-year-old wife; and farts at his rival. Alisoun also aspires to be courtly: 'Do way your hondes, for your curteysie', she says to the *hende* Nicholas. But her natural shrillness comes through when she says to Absolon: 'Go fro the window, Jakke fool'; and the rest of her conversation shows that she is as hard as Nicholas. Popular romances are conducted at a relentlessly high level of nobility, and do not contain the words *queynte, arse, piss* and *fart*; still less do they raise such questions as whether women have beards and where. Absolon aspires to live and love in the world of these romances: he protests that he cannot sleep; he '*rometh* to the carpenteres hous', serenades her, kneels for a kiss, asking for her *grace*. He falls short of the noble ideal, however, in his obsession with the sweetness of his breath, in his efforts to bribe Alisoun, and in every self-regarding word he utters. Only in his revenge does he show heroic qualities:

> This Nicholas anon leet fle a fart
> As greet as it had been a thonder-dent,
> That with the strook *he* was almost yblent;   [Absolon]

And he was redy with his iren hoot,
And Nicholas amidde the ers he smoot.

(698–702)

(This may parody the encounter between Palamon and Arcite in the *Knight's Tale*. 'Tho chaungen gan the colour in hir face...' (780–900).) But from his initial portrait we already knew that Absolon was a figure of fun, with his absurd *bouffant* hair-style and his pride in his *joly* parting. His red complexion and 'eyen greye as goos' are the standard attributes not of the hero but of the heroine of a romance.

The other kind of parody in the poem is related, in an upside-down way, to the Bible. Both the Bible and the romances offered noble if different ideals of conduct, religious and secular. But the romances offered ideals of conduct which at their best Chaucer suspected and at their silliest (in their popular forms) he laughed at. It is these popular romances which are aped in word and deed by Absolon and, in word only, by Nicholas. The models and examples offered by the Bible are casually mentioned very often in the *Tale* (witness the names of Pilate, Solomon, Absolon, Herod, Noe, God, Christ and Satan) but it does not occur to any of the characters to attempt to follow or avoid them. The parody of romance makes the romances (and Absolon) ludicrous; the parody or travesty of the Bible makes the characters, rather than the Bible, ridiculous. In particular, the story of the Annunciation and the passionate language of the Song of Songs are made present in the *Tale*, and the effect of this is to render the perverse antics of these fallen human beings grotesque and gargoyle-like as well as laughable. The parody of the Bible is situational as well as verbal (see discussions in Sections 3.5 and 3.6).

4.3 PUNS

The purely verbal skills of Chaucer are manifold in the *Miller's Tale*. The *Tale* is told with great verve and the colloquial smack of an orally-delivered performance, which is felt after the teller's own persona has been left behind. This is especially felt in passages of action ('off gooth the skin'), of direct speech ('Help us, seinte Frideswide') and of exclamatory comment ('She was a prymerole'; 'Lo, which a greet thyng is affeccioun'). It is the kind of poetry which completely conceals its poeticality. But there is also a more cunning, conscious and concentrated verbalism in the *Tale*, expressed in parody, travesty and in several kinds of plays on words such as malapropisms, puns and other in-jokes. We have noticed John's 'astromie' and 'Nowel', and the string of jokes on *hende, queynte, privetee* and *wood*. There is Abs*olon*/Pa*lamon* and Nichol*as*/*Arc*ite (in which there is, alas, a pun on 'arse': 'And Nicholas amid the arse he smoot'). Once the expectation of sexual *double entendre* has been created, of course, such jokes can be seen or imagined at every turn (or cat-hole). A more artistic touch can be seen in the variation Chaucer plays on *compaignye*. Introduced in line 96 in parody of the *Knight's Tale* (see Section 3.4), there is another allusion to it at line 601 ('*com pa me*', 'Kiss me quick'), a catch from a popular song or game; and a last at 731: 'par compaignye' – the young pair pretend to be kindly 'keeping John company'.

4.4 POETRY?

The *Miller's Tale* is skilfully told and well written, but is it poetry? Ezra Pound defined the nineteenth-century idea of poetry as 'beeyutiful thoughts in flowery langwidge'. Absolon would have agreed. Twentieth-century poetry is characteristically short and personal, and narratives are almost invariably written in prose. Chaucer uses prose for only two of the *Canterbury Tales*, his own *Tale of Melibee* (a moral allegory) and the *Parson's* so-called *Tale*, a tract on penitence. If we expect the language of poetry to be especially 'creative', imaginative and original, we are confining poetry to one of its extremes – the modern, lyrical, expressive and emotional extreme – and forgetting its former use for epic, drama, satire, epistle, narrative, entertainment and instruction. In the poetic theory of the Middle Ages (as before and after), poetry was a branch of rhetoric in which Decorum – the principle of suitability – was the first rule. The Miller is a churl, and therefore tells a churl's tale in a churl's manner – though such decorum is highly indecorous. The kinds of comic distortion of language we have seen – hyperbole, parody, malapropism, punning – are also appropriate to comedy, in which anarchy is, for a time, allowed its head. But of the kinds of poetic excellence which, since the Romantics, critics have particularly praised – the uses of language which appeal especially to the imagination – there is little in this *Tale* outside the formal portraits of Alisoun and Absolon; and the appeal of Alisoun's apple-like breath has led to her portrait being misinterpreted.

Imaginacioun is an untrustworthy guide to realistic conduct, as John and Absolon find out: John sees Noe's Flood come *Walwynge as the see/*

To drenchen Alisoun, his hony deere (507-8), and Absolon thinks she is as sweet as her image suggests. Nicholas uses his imagination to fuel John's fantasy of their surviving the second Flood: the pair will be as faithful as a white duck and her drake. In a humbler sense, imagery contributes greatly to the *Tale*, which is packed with bright, clear, physical pictures of the characters and, especially, of their setting. But this is not the rich imagery of the Romantic poets.

A specifically poetic feature of which use is made in the *Tale* is rhyme. The *Tale* is told in rhyming iambic pentameter couplets, the staple verse-form of the *Canterbury Tales*, used throughout Fragment A, in all the Headlinks and in many *Tales*. In the Renaissance and especially the Augustan periods, the rhyming couplet was used for heroic poetry and drama whence it became known as the heroic couplet; but also for satire. John Donne's *Satire III*, John Dryden's *Absalom and Achitophel*, Alexander Pope's *Rape of the Lock* and much else, and Samuel Johnson's *The Vanity of Human Wishes* are all composed in such couplets.

The couplet is well suited to convey statement and antithesis, and its immediate rhyme allows a clinching effect which can sharpen a point. Shakespeare used the couplet to close up a scene with a summary or a moral point, and it was he who made the couplet the standard ending for the English sonnet. In general, then, later English verse makes us familiar with the couplet as a vehicle for statement: the immediate rhyme has the effect of matching the lines, and writers tended to end the sense with the second line. The statement made in the couplet gathers from this finality a tendency to epigram, clarity, neatness, balance, antithesis and, at times, paradox.

Chaucer, in contrast, used it for narrative. He opens out the couplet, making the sense flow on through the second rhyme, and more often than not beginning a new sense-unit with the second line. To close the couplet would impede the natural colloquial energy of a low and realistic tale. Normally Chaucer makes us forget the couplet, and indeed forget versification and style altogether: his art was to conceal art. The state of the language, with its variable and at times optional final *e*, meant that lines had ten *or* eleven syllables, an irregularity which reduces symmetry and polish.

A typical passage showing the couplet's adaptability and flexibility might be lines 179-88:

> 'Do wey youre handes, for youre curteisie!'

> This Nicholas gan mercy for to crye,
> And spak so faire, and profred him so faste,

> That she hir love him graunted atte laste,
> And swoor hir ooth, by Seint Thomas of Kent,
> That she wol been at his comandement,
> Whan that she may hir leiser wel espie.

> 'Myn housbonde is so ful of jalousie
> That but ye waite wel and been privee,
> I woot right wel I nam but deed,' quod she.
> 'Ye moste been ful deerne, as in this cas.'

The middle sentence of this passage runs on easily through six lines with so much matter that we do not notice the manner. Only with the next line does Chaucer exploit the couplet's built-in capacity for emphasis:

> 'Nay, thereof care thee noght,' quod Nicholas.
> 'A clerk hadde litherly biset his while,
> But if he koude a carpenter bigile.'

Here Chaucer allows the natural antithesis of a couplet to develop between clerk and 'carpenter', and imparts to this last word all the exaggerated Oxford scorn of Gown for Town. The expressiveness of natural speech is well suggested by the contemptuous alliteration to bring out the contrast. The rhyme itself is not clinching, but the sense fits well into the couplet.

The first significant rhyme in the *Tale* is, just earlier, the notorious 'queynte' (167-8). Identical rhymes in differing senses were appreciated in the verse of the time; another example is the play on *stele* at 677-8. Identical rhyme is avoided today, perhaps as too strong a reminder of the arbitrariness of the connection between the signification of words and their sound. As there were no dictionaries in the Middle Ages, this arbitrariness was perhaps more evident. Chaucer was a careful craftsman and did not make a rhyme prominent without a purpose. Some rhymes are merely convenient: 'Absolon/anon' and 'Nicholas/cas' occur several times; the only significance of this is that Chaucer wishes to use their names prominently and often. But, against this norm of casualness, 'Nicholas/allas' (thrice) and 'Nicholas/solas' (twice) seem more pointed. 'Privetee' is a key word in the tale, as we know from its Prologue; it occurs in a rhyming position five times. The commonest rhyme in the tale is 'wyf/lyf', as in:

> This carpenter had wedded newe a wyf,
> Which that he lovede moore than his lyf. (113-4)

This uxorious rhyme occurs again at 33-4, 235-6, 413-4, 473-4 and 501-2. *Wyf* is also rhymed with 'inquisityf' (55) and 'stryf' (441 and 741). Other thematic rhymes are 'stood/wood' (327-8), 'wood/blood' (399-400) and 'wood/flood' (409-10, 709-10, 725-6). Notable rhymes are 'misse/kisse' (571-2) and the shocking 'kisse/pisse' (689-90). Final examples of the pointed use of rhyme are 'astromye/prye' (349-50), 'cinamome/to me' (591-2) and 'squaymous/daungerous' (229-30). In all of these three there is some witty association of incongruous ideas, ideas which have a bearing on important issues in the *Tale*. The second line frequently turns to anticlimax at the last word, as often in the satirical couplets of Dryden and Pope.

If poetry is the proper use of the powers and patterns of sound and sense natural in language, Chaucer certainly uses the full width of the language in the *Miller's Tale* – fresh, apt and vigorous English raised (for the most part) unnoticeably above casual speech, fluent and easy to a degree unknown in any later writer. There are set-pieces – portraits, speeches, passages of rapid dialogue or action – and also one or two stunts – puns, rhymes or parodies – but mostly Chaucer's distinction as a stylist is his ease, transparency, freshness and limpidity. This is what Edmund Spenser seized on when he called Chaucer a 'well of English undefyled'. Chaucer could write formal and beautiful poetry when required: his *Troilus and Criseyde* is the most beautiful long poem in English. Here he had a different task, to make a Miller tell his tale 'in his manere'.

5 SPECIMEN PASSAGE

AND COMMENTARY

5.1 SPECIMEN PASSAGE

Absolon (lines 204-30)

> Now was ther of that chirche a parissh clerk,
> The which that was ycleped Absolon.
> Crul was his heer, and as the gold it shoon,
> And strouted as a fanne large and brode;
> Ful streight and evene lay his joly shode.
> His rode was reed, his eyen greye as goos.
> With Poules window corven on his shoos,
> In hoses rede he wente fetisly.
>
> Yclad he was ful smal and proprely
> Al in a kirtel of a light waget;
> Ful faire and thikke been the pointes set.
> And therupon he hadde a gay surplis
> As whit as is the blosme upon the ris.
>
> A mirie child he was, so God me save.
> Wel koude he laten blood and clippe and shave,
> And maken a chartre of lond or acquitaunce.
> In twenty manere koude he trippe and daunce
> After the scole of Oxenforde tho,
> And with his legges casten to and fro,
> And pleyen songes on a smal rubible;
> Thereto he song som time a loud quinible;
> And as wel koude he pleye on a giterne.
> In al the toun nas brewhous ne taverne
> That he ne visited with his solas,

Ther any gailard tappestere was.
But sooth to seyn, he was somdeel squaymous
Of farting, and of speche daungerous.

5.2 COMMENTARY

The parish clerk's role, and character, and the import of his name, have
been touched on in Section 2.2, but a purely critical account of his
portrait may help us appreciate Chaucer's art. Compare the remarks on
the portraits of the Miller and Alisoun in Sections 2.2 and 3.2.

The portrait is a satirical one, and its essential technique is the
standard one of ironical praise. This is easy to see in 'A myrie child he
was, so God me save', where we have seen enough of Absolon to know
that the Miller's own reaction to him would not be along these lines.
Nor does the list of accomplishments given in explanation seem likely
to have appealed to the macho Miller.

From the outset the name Absolon, followed by 'Crul was his heer',
would signal a type of youthful masculine vanity. Chaucer's subtlety as
a satirist is that his ironical praise is not obvious and given from the outside, but seems to emanate from within the character; so that we
receive Absolon's own pleased opinion of himself, as if he were regarding
his figure in a full-length mirror. The description goes from top to toe
and then fills in the details of the clothing, much in the way of the
modern fashion page. It would be easy to find parallels for this portrait
in the work of the Italian painters who came after Chaucer, such as
Gentile da Fabriano, Pisanello, Paolo Uccello, Fra Angelico, Piero della
Francesca and Vittore Carpaccio. In the work of all these artists are to
be found portraits of sub-angelic young men, whether princes, courtiers,
pages, musicians, grooms or gondoliers, ravished by their own appearance. What is striking is not only the clarity of the fashionable detail,
but the profusion and the tone of the adjectives and adverbs:

> *Ful streight and evene* lay his *joly* shode. . .

> Yclad he was *ful smal and proprely*
> *Al* in a kirtel *of a light waget*;
> *Ful faire and thikke* been the pointes set.

(author's italics)

The passage is thick with sartorial detail but thicker still with exclamatory and fussy qualifiers, *full* of excitement, in a parody of a pansy

style. The concluding couplet emerges with a wonderful complacency:

> And thereupon he hadde a gay surplis
> As whit as is the blosme upon the ris.

Factually this means that his topmost garment was the white surplice which marks him as a parish clerk. But the epithet and the girlishly lyrical comparison transform this ordinary fact into an index of his inane frivolity and self-admiring silliness. His 'so-simple' surplice adds just the right touch of clerical innocence to his dandyism.

Absolon's accomplishments may strike us as oddly combined but must have been common enough as ways of getting pin-money for young clerics. They are menial and worldly, and *clippe and shave* continues the stress on hair which is Absolon's signature. His own hairstyle, the size and shape of a broad-mouthed winnowing basket, must have made him an object of attention even among the many students in a small town like Oxford; and in the public houses, an object of comment to the lively barmaids he serenaded. His behaviour is all designed to attract notice – morris dancing, singing, fiddle and guitar playing – and all remarkably unclerical. This goes without saying, and makes a contrast with the Clerk of Oxenford in the *General Prologue* and with the self-effacing but efficient Nicholas. Less obvious but equally important is an implied comparison with a real copybook courtly lover such as the Squire in the *General Prologue*, who is gaily dressed and sings all day, but does not cast his legs or eyes about; he has noble and manly accomplishments and is humbly attentive to his duties. Absolon is a small-town barber's assistant, a provincial peacock. The famous final couplet tailors him exactly for his fall; note that 'dangerous' is an adjective (lofty, aloof) applying to Absolon's manner of speech. He is squeamish about farting, and refined in speech.

In general, then, the portrait is a fine example of Chaucer's exuberant use of conventions. The name, the physical type, the minute social detail, all are familiar enough from the literature and art of the time. But Chaucer does not give us a stock character: Absolon is an invention, a lively and sophisticated creation, and his portrait prepares us for the rich elaboration of these stock ingredients (vanity, effeminacy, social pretension) in the action of the tale, in the complication of which he plays the leading part. What differentiates him from Nicholas and Alisoun is the extent to which we see him from within: we can immediately tell how intensely Absolon is pleased with himself. Although his portrait begins in caricature it rapidly takes off so that he almost becomes a personality. Chaucer, in effect, allows Absolon to present himself: so that we share his gleeful narcissism without ever forgetting how ineffably silly he is. In the end he is not a three-dimensional character, but after this portrait we have a developed idea not only of what he looks like but of exactly how he works. This helps us appreciate every nuance of his rise and fall, and even of his revenge. The portrait at first strikes us by the life of its details, but its true skill lies in the ease of its (apparently sympathetic) access to Absolon's image of himself.

6 CRITICAL RECEPTION

The *Miller's Tale* was not considered worthy of a critical reception until well into this century. Chaucer's contemporaries admired him first as a skilful writer of English; as a translator (of French poetry); and as a philosophical poet of love. In the Renaissance his eloquence and learning were again praised, and also his morality. John Dryden, the first true critic to write on Chaucer at any length (in his *Preface* to the *Fables*, published in 1700), admired the poet's 'wonderful comprehensiveness of nature'. Of the *Canterbury Tales* he said famously, 'here is God's plenty', and in the *Fables* he put some of the *Tales* into modern English; but he omitted the *fabliaux* as indecent, though he admitted they would amuse many readers. It was at the end of the seventeenth century that the popular image of Chaucer as a 'merry', rather rude, poet began to gain currency. In his youthful *Imitations of the Poets* Alexander Pope chose pseudo-Chaucerian couplets as the proper vehicle for a bawdy little story. And it was at this time that the *Tales* came to replace *Troilus and Criseyde* as Chaucer's most popular work.

William Wordsworth tells us in *The Prelude* that he laughed over Chaucer; and his sister Dorothy wrote in her journal for Boxing Day 1801: 'After tea we sate by the fire comfortably. I read aloud – The Miller's Tale.' The later nineteenth century was to appreciate the tender pathos in which Chaucer specialised (though not in the *Miller's Tale*) rather than the robust humour which the eighteenth century had enjoyed in him. Matthew Arnold, the best critic of Chaucer after Dryden, found him wanting in 'high seriousness'. It is true that he often lacks a settled and elevated tone.

But one of the many recent American academic critics of Chaucer defined seriousness 'not as a matter of subject, but of treatment, of careful attention to getting the thing said in the best possible way. Has not Mr. T. S. Eliot told us that Villon's *Testament* is more serious than *In Memoriam*? In the same sense the *Miller's Tale* is more serious than the *Knight's Tale*. . .' (P. F. Baum in Burrow, *Geoffrey Chaucer*, p. 189). In his chapter on 'The Fabliaux' in Beryl Rowland's *Companion to Chaucer Studies* D. S. Brewer shows how these low stories considered by earlier critics as amusing, negligible or offensive, have 'rocketed into a position of central importance for most critics of Chaucer.' 'Rocketed' is not too strong a word for this development when one considers that the respected editor J. M. Manly omitted all the *fabliaux* from his monumental edition of *The Canterbury Tales* in 1940. The *Miller's Tale*, for long read under the school desk with whoops of laughter, is now an examination set text.

The reasons for this revolution in taste lie deeper than fashions among academics and school examiners, but it is a curious fact that many of the best academic critics have done their best with the *Miller's Tale*. None of them is, as a critic, a central figure in our literary culture, and they are none of them as humane in their writings on Chaucer, or as quotable, as John Dryden, William Blake, Matthew Arnold or even G. K. Chesterton or Ezra Pound, but in their minuteness they are more helpful as examples to essay-writers; and the pages by C. Muscatine and E. Talbot Donaldson mentioned in 'Further Reading' are impressive examples of professional criticism.

It is also remarkable that although Chaucer has in this century attracted a great deal of attention from literary critics and scholars, especially in American universities, he has not in England been fully assimilated by critics into the literary tradition at the head of which he undoubtedly stands. In the sixteenth century, Edmund Spenser imitated Chaucer's language, and William Shakespeare drew plots from Chaucer for two of his plays; and in the seventeenth century John Dryden modernised some of Chaucer's tales. But in the eighteenth century the Middle Ages were generally not taken seriously – they were derided as barbarous, ignorant and superstitious. The revival of mediaeval things by such authors as Thomas Gray, Thomas Chatterton and Sir Walter Scott had to recreate a mediaeval world of romance which was Romantic partly because it was unknown and alien. Although in the nineteenth century scholars eventually recovered for us a much more accurate idea of Chaucer's language and of his world, he was still, when read as a whole, felt to be mediaeval, not modern, different.

The *General Prologue* to the *Canterbury Tales* is something of an exception to this, perhaps because it is apparently realistic in style, and a few of the *Tales*, such as those of the Nun's Priest, the Pardoner and also the Miller, have continued to be read and enjoyed. A vulgarised theatrical version of the *Canterbury Tales* ran for several years in the West End of London in the 1960s and 1970s. But there is now a yawning gap between this simple, old-fashioned Chaucer and the sophisticated Chaucer of some modern academic critics.

In the teaching of English literature in schools and universities there is a deep-rooted notion of English literary history as beginning with the Renaissance at the court of King Henry VIII, with such poets as Sir Thomas Wyatt and Henry Howard, Earl of Surrey, and flowering in the reign of Queen Elizabeth I with the writings of Sir Philip Sidney, Edmund Spenser, Christopher Marlowe and William Shakespeare. This later Tudor flowering roughly coincided with the establishment of a national State and a national Church, a conscious Englishness; it also coincided with the formation of a national language, because what we call Modern English begins in Tudor times, which is why we can still read Shakespeare and the Authorized Version of the Bible (dating from 1611) with only local difficulties. There had been many great changes in the structure of the English language in the fifteenth century, which now make the reading of Chaucer much more difficult, although easier than with nearly all of his contemporaries.

The removal of England from mediaeval Christendom makes for cultural differences between the modern reader and Chaucer which are quite as important as the linguistic differences. It is possible to feel cultural difference within a broader cultural continuity, a feeling which lends piquancy to the reading of Chaucer. But there is little doubt that the changes referred to here have successively brought different aspects of Chaucer into prominence: the eloquent, the philosophical, the moral, the comic, the pathetic, the realistic. The rise of English literature to the apex of the arts syllabus in modern education came to require improving and enriching qualities in our classic authors. The Victorian Matthew Arnold found Chaucer a tonic; but not steadily sublime and serious enough for him to qualify for true greatness. But Arnold could see Chaucer as part of the European tradition of Homer, Virgil and Dante. F. R. Leavis, the influential Cambridge twentieth-century critic, helped to establish for many teachers of English a more parochial and earnest notion of a peculiarly English literary tradition, a modern tradition beginning with Shakespeare. One inadequacy of this outlook is suggested by the remark of one of Leavis's followers, John Spiers, quoted below.

The elevated, playful or pathetic Chaucer represented by the *Knight's, Nun's Priest's* or *Franklin's Tales* is now joined in popularity by the more broadly humorous and 'realistic' Chaucer of the *Miller's Tale*. This is partly due to the breakdown in the 1960s of the notion that classic literature is always respectable. But the *Miller's Tale* remains, if not a great work of art, a highly enjoyable work of great art, full of life and not without life's complexity.

Some selected remarks: 'The working-out of the *Miller's Tale* is attended by feelings akin to those of religious wonder' (E. M. W. Tillyard). 'The universe no longer appearing to have a moral structure, we seek morality in, of all places, Fabliaux' (D. S. Brewer). 'From these images [in the portrait of Alisoun] springs directly the recognition that her potentialities are simply those of nature, of a natural creature, wild, young, untamed' (John Speirs).

REVISION QUESTIONS

1. Compare the portraits of the three young lovers and draw conclusions.

2. What is the moral of the *Miller's Tale*, if any?

3. Discuss the religious references in the *Miller's Tale* and the uses to which they are put.

4. Discuss the use of settings *or* parody *or* plot *or* characterisation by speech in the *Miller's Tale*.

5. Discuss the contrasts between words and deeds in the *Miller's Tale*.

6. What does the *Miller's Tale* gain from its being in verse?

7. How does the *Miller's Tale*'s immediate context in the *Canterbury Tales* help us to interpret it?

8. 'The *Miller's Tale* is an elaborate dirty joke and no more. It cannot be considered as literature.' Give a carefully argued response to this reaction.

FURTHER READING

Text

The *Miller's Tale* is part of the First Fragment (lines 1–4422) of the *Canterbury Tales*, comprising the *General Prologue* and the *Tales* of the Knight, Miller, Reeve and Cook together with their linking material. This Fragment should be read, and is best read in the standard edition for reference, *The Works of Geoffrey Chaucer*, edited by F. N. Robinson (2nd edn, Oxford University Press, 1957). The edition of the *Canterbury Tales* by A. C. Cawley (Dent, 1958) has marginal glosses of hard words. The only edition of the *Miller's Tale* currently available is by J. Winny (Cambridge University Press, 1971). Quotations and line numbers are taken from Winny's text, which is itself taken from Robinson's edition. A third edition of Robinson is in preparation, with an on-the-page glossary, and this should prove of great use.

General background

Brewer, Derek, *Chaucer and his World* (Eyre Methuen, 1978).
⠀⠀⠀⠀⠀⠀⠀⠀*English Gothic Literature* (Macmillan, 1983).
Coghill, Nevill, *The Poet Chaucer* (2nd edn, Oxford University Press, 1968).
Ford, Boris (ed.), *The New Pelican Guide to English Literature, vol 1: Medieval Literature, Part 1: Chaucer and the Alliterative Tradition; Part 2: The European Inheritance* (Penguin, 1983).
Rowland, Beryl (ed.), *Companion to Chaucer Studies* (Oxford University Press, 1968). Especially the chapter on *The Fabliaux* by D. S. Brewer.

Criticism

Burrow, J. A. (ed.), *Geoffrey Chaucer: A Critical Anthology* (Penguin,

1969). Especially the contributions by C. Muscatine and R. E. Kaske.

Kolve, V. A., *Chaucer and the Imagery of Narrative* (Arnold, 1984).

Muscatine, C., *Chaucer and the French Tradition* (Cambridge University Press, 1957). See pages 223–30 on the *Miller's Tale* (also reprinted in Burrow, above).

Ross, T. W. (ed), *A Variorum Edition of the Works of Geoffrey Chaucer, vol 2: The Canterbury Tales, Part 3: The Miller's Tale* (University of Oklahoma Press, 1983).

Schoeck, R. and Taylor, J. (eds), *Chaucer Criticism*, vol 1 (University of Notre Dame Press, 1960). See pages 117–29, 'Characterization in the Miller's Tale' by P. E. Beichner.

Donaldson, E. Talbot, *Speaking of Chaucer* (Athlone Press, 1970). Especially the chapter 'Idiom of Popular Poetry in the *Miller's Tale*'.

Records and tapes

The Miller's Prologue and Tale read by A. C. Spearing (Cambridge University Press). Reel 211840; cassette 21185 9.

The Miller's Tale, read in Middle English by Norman Davis (Tellways) Cassette TWC 3.

The Miller's Tale and *The Reeve's Tale*, read in Middle English by J. B. Bessinger Jr. (Caedmon) TC 1223.

Medieval English Lyrics (Argo Record Company Limited, London). Especially the English version of Nicholas's song, 'Angelus ad virginem'.

The Miller's Tale, read in Middle English by N. F. Blake and A. B. Burnley (Audio Learning Educational) ELA 986 (cassette).

Mastering English Literature
Richard Gill

Mastering English Literature will help readers both to enjoy English Literature and to be successful in 'O' levels, 'A' levels and other public exams. It is an introduction to the study of poetry, novels and drama which helps the reader in four ways - by providing ways of approaching literature, by giving examples and practice exercises, by offering hints on how to write about literature, and by the author's own evident enthusiasm for the subject. With extracts from more than 200 texts, this is an enjoyable account of how to get the maximum satisfaction out of reading, whether it be for formal examinations or simply for pleasure.

Work Out English Literature ('A' level)
S.H. Burton

This book familiarises 'A' level English Literature candidates with every kind of test which they are likely to encounter. Suggested answers are worked out step by step and accompanied by full author's commentary. The book helps students to clarify their aims and establish techniques and standards so that they can make appropriate responses to similar questions when the examination pressures are on. It opens up fresh ways of looking at the full range of set texts, authors and critical judgements and motivates students to know more of these matters.

Also from Macmillan

CASEBOOK SERIES

The Macmillan *Casebook* series brings together the best of modern criticism with a selection of early reviews and comments. Each Casebook charts the development of opinion on a play, poem, or novel, or on a literary genre, from its first appearance to the present day.

GENERAL THEMES

COMEDY: DEVELOPMENTS IN CRITICISM
D. J. Palmer

DRAMA CRITICISM: DEVELOPMENTS SINCE IBSEN
A. J. Hinchliffe

THE ENGLISH NOVEL: DEVELOPMENTS IN CRITICISM SINCE HENRY JAMES
Stephen Hazell

THE LANGUAGE OF LITERATURE
N. Page

THE PASTORAL MODE
Bryan Loughrey

THE ROMANTIC IMAGINATION
J. S. Hill

TRAGEDY: DEVELOPMENTS IN CRITICISM
R. P. Draper

POETRY

WILLIAM BLAKE: SONGS OF INNOCENCE AND EXPERIENCE
Margaret Bottrall

BROWNING: MEN AND WOMEN AND OTHER POEMS
J. R. Watson

BYRON: CHILDE HAROLD'S PILGRIMAGE AND DON JUAN
John Jump

CHAUCER: THE CANTERBURY TALES
J. J. Anderson

COLERIDGE: THE ANCIENT MARINER AND OTHER POEMS
A. R. Jones and W. Tydeman

DONNE: SONGS AND SONETS
Julian Lovelock

T. S. ELIOT: FOUR QUARTETS
Bernard Bergonzi

T. S. ELIOT: PRUFROCK, GERONTION, ASH WEDNESDAY AND OTHER POEMS
B. C. Southam

T. S. ELIOT: THE WASTELAND
C. B. Cox and A. J. Hinchliffe

ELIZABETHAN POETRY: LYRICAL AND NARRATIVE
Gerald Hammond

THOMAS HARDY: POEMS
J. Gibson and T. Johnson

GERALD MANLEY HOPKINS: POEMS
Margaret Bottrall

KEATS: ODES
G. S. Fraser

KEATS: THE NARRATIVE POEMS
J. S. Hill

MARVELL: POEMS
Arthur Pollard

THE METAPHYSICAL POETS
Gerald Hammond

MILTON: PARADISE LOST
A. E. Dyson and Julian Lovelock

POETRY OF THE FIRST WORLD
WAR
Dominic Hibberd

ALEXANDER POPE: THE RAPE OF
THE LOCK
John Dixon Hunt

SHELLEY: SHORTER POEMS &
LYRICS
Patrick Swinden

SPENSER: THE FAERIE QUEEN
Peter Bayley

TENNYSON: IN MEMORIAM
John Dixon Hunt

THIRTIES POETS: 'THE AUDEN
GROUP'
Ronald Carter

WORDSWORTH: LYRICAL
BALLADS
A. R. Jones and W. Tydeman

WORDSWORTH: THE PRELUDE
W. J. Harvey and R. Gravil

W. B. YEATS: POEMS 1919–1935
E. Cullingford

W. B. YEATS: LAST POEMS
Jon Stallworthy

THE NOVEL AND PROSE

JANE AUSTEN: EMMA
David Lodge

JANE AUSTEN: NORTHANGER
ABBEY AND PERSUASION
B. C. Southam

JANE AUSTEN: SENSE AND
SENSIBILITY, PRIDE AND
PREJUDICE AND MANSFIELD
PARK
B. C. Southam

CHARLOTTE BRONTË: JANE EYRE
AND VILLETTE
Miriam Allott

EMILY BRONTË: WUTHERING
HEIGHTS
Miriam Allott

BUNYAN: THE PILGRIM'S
PROGRESS
R. Sharrock

CONRAD: HEART OF DARKNESS,
NOSTROMO AND UNDER
WESTERN EYES
C. B. Cox

CONRAD: THE SECRET AGENT
Ian Watt

CHARLES DICKENS: BLEAK
HOUSE
A. E. Dyson

CHARLES DICKENS: DOMBEY
AND SON AND LITTLE DORRITT
Alan Shelston

CHARLES DICKENS: HARD TIMES,
GREAT EXPECTATIONS AND OUR
MUTUAL FRIEND
N. Page

GEORGE ELIOT: MIDDLEMARCH
Patrick Swinden

GEORGE ELIOT: THE MILL ON
THE FLOSS AND SILAS MARNER
R. P. Draper

HENRY FIELDING: TOM JONES
Neil Compton

E. M. FORSTER: A PASSAGE TO
INDIA
Malcolm Bradbury

HARDY: THE TRAGIC NOVELS
R. P. Draper

HENRY JAMES: WASHINGTON
SQUARE AND THE PORTRAIT OF
A LADY
Alan Shelston

JAMES JOYCE: DUBLINERS AND A
PORTRAIT OF THE ARTIST AS A
YOUNG MAN
Morris Beja

D. H. LAWRENCE: THE RAINBOW
AND WOMEN IN LOVE
Colin Clarke

D. H. LAWRENCE: SONS AND
LOVERS
Gamini Salgado

SWIFT: GULLIVER'S TRAVELS
Richard Gravil

THACKERAY: VANITY FAIR
Arthur Pollard

TROLLOPE: THE BARSETSHIRE
NOVELS
T. Bareham

VIRGINIA WOOLF: TO THE
LIGHTHOUSE
Morris Beja

DRAMA

CONGREVE: COMEDIES
Patrick Lyons

T. S. ELIOT: PLAYS
Arnold P. Hinchliffe

JONSON: EVERY MAN IN HIS
HUMOUR AND THE ALCHEMIST
R. V. Holdsworth

JONSON: VOLPONE
J. A. Barish

MARLOWE: DR FAUSTUS
John Jump

MARLOWE: TAMBURLAINE,
EDWARD II AND THE JEW OF
MALTA
John Russell Brown

MEDIEVAL ENGLISH DRAMA
Peter Happé

O'CASEY: JUNO AND THE
PAYCOCK, THE PLOUGH AND THE
STARS AND THE SHADOW OF A
GUNMAN
R. Ayling

JOHN OSBORNE: LOOK BACK IN
ANGER
John Russell Taylor

WEBSTER: THE WHITE DEVIL AND
THE DUCHESS OF MALFI
R. V. Holdsworth

WILDE: COMEDIES
W. Tydeman

SHAKESPEARE

SHAKESPEARE: ANTONY AND
CLEOPATRA
John Russell Brown

SHAKESPEARE: CORIOLANUS
B. A. Brockman

SHAKESPEARE: HAMLET
John Jump

SHAKESPEARE: HENRY IV PARTS
I AND II
G. K. Hunter

SHAKESPEARE: HENRY V
Michael Quinn

SHAKESPEARE: JULIUS CAESAR
Peter Ure

SHAKESPEARE: KING LEAR
Frank Kermode

SHAKESPEARE: MACBETH
John Wain

SHAKESPEARE: MEASURE FOR
MEASURE
G. K. Stead

SHAKESPEARE: THE MERCHANT
OF VENICE
John Wilders

SHAKESPEARE: A MIDSUMMER
NIGHT'S DREAM
A. W. Price

SHAKESPEARE: MUCH ADO
ABOUT NOTHING AND AS YOU
LIKE IT
John Russell Brown

SHAKESPEARE: OTHELLO
John Wain

SHAKESPEARE: RICHARD II
N. Brooke

SHAKESPEARE: THE SONNETS
Peter Jones

SHAKESPEARE: THE TEMPEST
D. J. Palmer

SHAKESPEARE: TROILUS AND
CRESSIDA
Priscilla Martin

SHAKESPEARE: TWELFTH NIGHT
D. J. Palmer

SHAKESPEARE: THE WINTER'S
TALE
Kenneth Muir